The Wonder of Africa's Natural History

T0244028

The Wonder of
Africa's Natural History

Clive A. Spinage DSc

Whittles Publishing

Published by
Whittles Publishing Ltd,
Dunbeath,
Caithness, KW6 6EG,
Scotland, UK

www.whittlespublishing.com

© 2023 Clive A. Spinage

ISBN 978-184995-534-8

All photographs have been taken by the author, except for
Figure 25: Giraffe evolution. (Image: d'Ache, Caran. n.d. (c. 1900). Album
Caran d'Ache. album deuxième. Paris: Librairie Plon. p. 30.)
Figure 78; A billiard ball mountain representing the death of 1,140 elephants per year. (Photo:
Burroughes & Watts. n.d. (1889). *Billiards Simplified*. London: Burroughes & Watts.)

Printed and bound by CPI Group (UK) Ltd, Croydon, CR0 4YY

Contents

Preface

We cannot begin to comprehend the wonders of the natural world, the infinite intricacies of nature bound together in a world of beauty – wonder indeed! And when we think of that vast mysterious continent of Africa, we gasp with surprise at the great migrations of the Serengeti plains with their countless animals, or the sudden rush of a carnivore on its unsuspecting prey. But this is merely the surface of life that we are witnessing, a panorama of wonder embracing an infinite number of living creatures, ranging from strange parasites to bizarre insects and beautiful butterflies and birds, performing before a wondrous backdrop of vegetation from dry, seemingly inhospitable, grasslands to dense tropical forest overshadowed by giant trees. The wild creatures of the earth have ever had a fascination for us.

'An inexhaustible book of nature' was how a 19th-century writer described the English countryside – but how much more so are the wonders of Africa and its natural world with its incredible variety of life. You never know what will turn up next, and, as Sir Percy Fitzpatrick put it in his classic *Jock of the Bushveld* about life in the South African bush, the only certainty is that it won't be what you are expecting. From microscopic organisms that can kill, to mighty elephants roaming its wastes, Africa is the cradle of an astonishing array of animals, and with its plants it leaves one looking on in amazement at the infinite pattern of Nature.

To try to understand it we must be possessed of an enquiring mind, and my own vision of Africa has always been guided by an insatiable curiosity. How do these animals live? How do they behave? What do they think? Scientists are taught that they must be detached, and that we must not apply human attributes to wild animals. But it is hard to follow this advice when we watch wild animals in their natural habitat. The lazy doe waterbuck (was she really lazy?) I watched at dawn one day in Africa, who waited until the rest of her group, after getting to their feet, had wandered almost out of sight beginning their daily grazing round, before she reluctantly (was she really reluctant?) arose with an air of profound resignation (there I go again, breaking the rule; how could a wild animal have an air of resignation?), and slowly followed the others. We see affection among lions, we see anger. But are these human attributes we are ascribing to them?

The main object of study is, in my opinion, to enjoy it. So come with me as an enquiring naturalist, and let us try to fathom some of the secrets of Africa's wildlife, embarking on the greatest hunt of all, the hunt for knowledge.

1

How it all began:
the Mother of Monsters

L ittle more than one twentieth of Africa, East Africa's 1,761,000 square kilometres, of which 103,600 are water, boasts the richest animal array of the entire continent. In one day alone it is possible to see one thirty-fifth of the world's total bird species. Of some 8,600 in the world, Africa alone has 1,500, and East Africa at least half of this total.

There are some twice as many species of freshwater fish as there are bird species. Of the world's 15,000 fish species, Africa is home to about 2,900, and at least 900 of these occur in East Africa, with the majority of the remainder in the Congo Basin. But more than 600 consist of small fishes, known as cichlids, in Lake Malawi, and some people consider that as many again of these occur in Lake Victoria – remarkable fishes which have undergone an astonishing diversification.

Of at least 9,500 known reptile species in the world, Africa has some 1,320, including seven crocodiles; South America has some 1,560 reptile species, and Eurasia some 2,080. For a long time only three types of crocodile were believed to exist: the Nile, the dwarf, and the slender-snouted. Although at least five different species once co-existed around Kenya's Lake Turkana only the Nile crocodile lives there today. Genetics have now shown that the West African or desert crocodile is distinct from the Nile crocodile, which is more closely related to the American crocodiles, whilst the dwarf crocodile has three species, and the slender-snouted two species. Of some 6,770 amphibian species in the world – the frogs and toads, newts, and salamanders, and the legless, worm-like caecilians – Africa has the second-highest number of species (after South America), with some 622 species south of the Sahara, and more than 22 caecilians; but there are no salamanders or newts. Frogs and toads like relatively cool environments, so in the tropics they tend to be most numerous on mountains where the temperature is lower, and in the cooler Cape region they favour the lowlands.

Although in Britain we think of frogs as creatures of the aquatic environment, they can in fact live in deserts; one species coats its skin with a waxy secretion to avoid drying out, and excretes semi-solid urine. Some species even lay their eggs on land to develop directly into frogs without a tadpole stage. The largest frog is the goliath from West Africa, weighing in at 3.25 kilos and over 30 cm in length, whilst the smallest appears to be the rare micro or Cape Flats frog from the Western Cape, only 15 mm long. The goliath is a third larger than the African bullfrog, which is about 20 cm long, the females being larger than the males. Many frogs and toads have poisonous substances in their skin which are often copies of mammalian hormones, and which usually make any predator which samples them ill without killing it; but the predator remembers not to try again. One of the few investigated for this remarkable trait is the red-legged kassina, its red legs a warning to any predator. One of its poisons lowers the predator's blood pressure and stimulates vomiting, and another makes it violently ill. Only infinitesimal amounts are required to have an effect. That found in the skin of the guttural toad may be fatal to a consumer.

Mammals are less numerous, but East Africa has about one tenth of the world's estimated 4,500 species. This is a generous share, but one would be hardly likely to see more than twenty species in one day, as the greater part of this number is made up of small rodents. But then, could a sighting of twenty species in one day be equalled elsewhere in the world?

Let us not forget the insects. Out of a world estimate of some 5.5 million insects and 1.5 million beetles (plus another 7 million arthropods – spiders, ticks, and the like), more than 100,000 occur in sub-Saharan Africa. Of this sub-Saharan total there are some 2,674 butterfly species out of a world total of some 174,260, and of this sub-Saharan total the Congo alone has some 2,040, and Kenya 560. There are no estimates of the total number of beetles (the group which the scientist J B S Haldane once said God must be inordinately fond of because of their numbers) for Africa, but probably most occur in the Congo. But the most numerous insect must be the termite, believed to comprise 10 per cent of all animal weight; their conversion of plant material is considered equal to that of all the mammalian herbivores and fire put together. Voracious consumers of wood and dry vegetation, termites pepper the ground beneath your feet, betrayed by little holes in the surface, but more conspicuous in dry areas are their tall, chimney-like structures rearing from their mounds up to an astonishing almost 5 metres in height. These tall chimneys are to keep the inside of the mounds cool. In wetter areas the mounds assume intriguing shapes capped with little covers, some with a series of them, like Indonesian temples. The mounds protect the large grub-like queen, who may be over 6 cm long in some species, and whose sole role is to produce some 10 million eggs a year, attended by her king, soldiers, and workers. Some of these eggs produce winged kings and queens that fly from the mounds at the first rain and, after a brief nuptial flight in which mating takes place, come to ground and lose their wings, then burrow underground to try and form new colonies. Some species cultivate fungi gardens to feed on in their mounds.

And then there is Africa's eastern seaboard where in 1938, in the depths of the warm Indian Ocean that laps its shores, a remarkable fish was found, the coelacanth, 'old four-legs' with its four belly fins on stumps like legs, thought to have become extinct 66 million years ago. It is related to the archaic lungfish, a common freshwater fish in Uganda. Colourful tropical fishes abound in the coastal waters, and myriads of scavenging crabs continually race the tides across the sandy beaches.

[Clockwise from left]

A termite mound chimney in northern Kenya.

A quaintly shaped termite mound in the Central African Republic.

A pagoda-like termite mound in the Central African Republic.

East Africa's animals are a part of the Ethiopian sector of Wallace's Realms, named after the eminent Victorian zoologist who divided the world into six great zoogeographical realms. Despite the knowledge gained since Wallace's day, little change to his boundaries has been admitted. His understanding of the African fauna was remarkable, for at the time, based on the observations and collections of but a handful of explorers, the vast hinterland of Africa was little known.

Wallace divided the Ethiopian sector, that part of Africa lying south of the Tropic of Cancer and roughly excluding the Sahara, into the West, East, and South African regions, with Madagascar as a separate entity. The major change today is that the South and East African regions are considered as one.

East Africa's wealth of wildlife can be attributed to the fact that a great part of northern Africa is desert; central and west Africa is tropical rainforest, rich in plants and in sects; to the southwest of the continent desert intervenes again; whilst southern Africa is dry with cold winters. The eastern block of Kenya, Uganda, Tanzania, Mozambique, and Zambia has the best of all worlds; it is dry, but there is little desert, for the vast inland body of Lake Victoria keeps the interior moist. Those parts lying astride the equator are not subject to seasonal extremes

[Left] A Buffon's kob in burnt grassland in the Central African Republic.

[Below] The red fire mite emerges on burnt ground.

[Right] The brilliant
scarlet blooms
of the fire lily.

[Below] Fire burning in
woodland, Tanzania.

[Left] The red-hot poker tree with its flamboyant tufts of scarlet blossoms.

[Below] On the high mountains bizarre giant groundsels and lobelias are found.

of temperature, and have two rainy seasons, a long one and a short one; and the dry season is not cold, as it is in the south. To the east, the warm seaboard of the Indian Ocean has rain-bearing monsoons periodically blowing inland, and the country inland has plenty of broken high ground, providing a variety of habitats. The plains are subject to marked changes in the wet and the dry seasons: at the end of the dry much may go up in flames leaving a blackened desert, but bursting through the parched iron-hard soil, patches of ground are dazzling with their brilliant scarlet blooms of the fire lily, its scarlet warning that it is poisonous; indeed it may be used in arrow poison. But somehow animals seem to escape the fires, and with the first rains, which follow soon after, the plains burst into life again. Creatures such as the red velvet mite or rain bug crawl over the moist blackened surface. Looking like a little jewel, its bright scarlet warns of its unpleasant taste, although it is harmless to humans. The young stages are parasitic but the adults are carnivorous. Another scarlet wonder flowering in the dry season is the red-hot poker tree, with its flamboyant tufts of scarlet blossoms.

There is forest, but mainly of the dry mountain type, with trees such as East African 'cedar', a juniper once popular for pencil-making, and the tall podo trees, which produce very good furniture timber. Absence of a continuous rainfall means there is no tropical rainforest until we reach western Uganda, where rainfall is heavier and a more tropical aspect is found. Many of the trees here are buttressed; giant ferns occur, and tall grasses. On the high mountains bizarre giant groundsels and lobelias are found. But the typical vegetation of East Africa is fire-maintained; open park-like grassy plains, dotted with umbrella-shaped acacia thorn trees.

Mountain vegetation in Rwanda with giant groundsel and giant lobelia.

These vegetation types have co-existed for millions of years, with only their relative areas and dispositions changing from time to time. Some of these changes have been quite remarkable. Until recently it was believed, in spite of everything else, that the Congo Rainforest was one of the really permanent features of Africa. A product of several million years' stability. But with the discovery that almost the whole of it grows on sand blown in from the Kalahari desert this illusion has been shattered; we know now that about 50,000 years ago what is now the Congo Basin was desert. Then came another incursion of desert 40,000 years later, when the whole of southern Africa was very dry.

Still earlier, about 250 million years ago, what we now know as Africa was part of a single great global land mass, Pangaea, which split into two: Laurasia in the north and Gondwana in the south. Gondwana then began to split up about 115 million years ago. Gigantic land masses moved apart, South America breaking away about 100 million years ago, leaving Africa shifting northwards and in the process nearly losing the part lying east of the Rift Valley. Becoming isolated on all sides about 80 million years ago, its northward progress halted about 37 million years ago when it bumped into Eurasia, forcing up the Atlas mountains. It then pulled away from Eurasia about 23 million years ago, only to join up again about 17 million years ago, a huge sea known as Tethys being closed off to form the Mediterranean, from which point a number of Eurasian mammals seized the opportunity to move into Africa. These great movements of continents, known as continental drift, have now been refined into the theory of Tectonic Activity. The movement of the continents is caused by the movement of tectonic plates, massive slabs of rock under the continents and oceans, floating on the hot, toffee-like mantle, and moved around by its convective currents, some of the heavier plates sinking beneath the lighter ones, a movement which is still ongoing.

The displacement of the continents had isolated Africa long before the great burst of mammalian evolution started, but it was to be another 70 million years before the mammals began to show themselves in any strength. Only the African lungfish, *Protopterus*, survives in Africa today as a descendant of Gondwanaland's ancestors, with the exception of old four-legs in the depths of the Indian Ocean; most of Africa's vertebrates are more like those of Eurasia than Gondwanaland. A period of long isolation led to the evolution of a group comprising the elephants, hyraces, dugongs and manatees, aardvarks, and others, Africa's characteristic fauna appearing after 23 million years ago.

In the latter part of this Eocene period Africa saw many climatic and geological changes, but although sounding much more impressive, the geological events probably played only a minor part in affecting the animals and plants.

In 1921 J W Gregory wrote in his book *The Rift Valleys and Geology of East Africa*:

> The size of the area buried under volcanic material, the vast bulk of the ejecta, the variety of lavas, and the prolonged duration of the eruptions, make East Africa one of the greatest volcanic regions of the world. [Eruptions burst out on a] colossal scale ... deluging the country under floods of molten lava.

I doubt it was as dramatic as this, for the eruptions to which Gregory refers would have extended for over 70 million years. So there must have been long periods of inactivity interrupted by isolated eruptions that would have been unlikely to have more than local effects, with the exceptions of Mounts Kenya and Kilimanjaro, the latter a volcano of inconceivable size, but perhaps, again, it built up its mass bit by bit. Due to slow weathering the oldest volcanoes still stand side by side with the youngest, producing a landscape unrivalled for geological spectacle.

But it was the climatic, not geological, changes that exerted the greatest effects. Fluctuations of wet and dry repeatedly expanded and contracted deserts and forests, with a consequent shuttling to and fro of animal populations adapted to forest on the one hand and open grassland on the other.

Today East Africa provides a mosaic of almost every different habitat one can think of, with its ice-covered alpine slopes and the mountains' Jack-and-the-bean-stalk giant lobelias and giant senecios, now known as *dendrosenecio* or 'old man tree', allied to the sunflower and humble troublesome garden weed, groundsel; forests, grasslands, deserts, tropic palm-fringed shady shores, and coral beaches. Such diversity is reflected in the rich range of colonizers occupying this multitude of habitats. To understand how this wealth of life has come about, let us look at some of the remarkable animals that inhabited Africa in the past, fully justifying the ancients' title for the continent, the 'Mother of Monsters'.

2

From dinosaur to dik-dik

Had the climate of Africa remained stable for 100 million years, perhaps it would have been dinosaurs that met the guns of the Dutch in South Africa, not the quaggas and bluebuck that were shot to extinction. Although dinosaurs had been doomed to extinction by other hazards, they were by no means the first terrestrial vertebrates of note; preceding them by 90 million years in Africa were the mammal-like reptiles or synapsids, 'fused arch', the name relating to their skull structure: the most important fossil vertebrates ever discovered. They owe their importance to being the ancestors of our mammals, and they show us how a mammal evolved from a reptile. None reached great size; at most they were 3 to 4.5 metres in length, so they never attained a size that accords with the popular image of the dinosaurs. But their fossil record is more complete than that of any other group of terrestrial vertebrates, with the exception of the mammals of what we call the Tertiary period, the Pliocene to the Pleistocene geological ages, those two respectively starting 5 million and 2.6 million years ago.

The history of the earth is divided into geological periods, or ages, based upon what the rocks are made of, and the earliest synapsids occurred in the geological ages of the Upper Carboniferous, 359 million years ago, and Early Permian, 299 million years ago, in North America, with some in isolated spots in Europe. The first group to emerge in Africa were the therapsids, 'beast faces', referring to the same skull structure as that of the synapsids. They were connected via Russia with North American ancestors, the pelycosaurs, 'bowl lizards', which bore a sail-like crest along the back. The focus then shifted to what is now southern Africa; of course these countries were then all part of the single land mass, Pangea.

Not the least surprising about the therapsids is that in less than half a square kilometre of the South African Karoo, you could find the fossils of around a hundred or more of these 250 million-year-old animals just lying on the surface. They evolved into literally millions of species: insectivorous, carnivorous, herbivorous, and omnivorous.

The carnivores, about the size of a hyaena and with the hyaena's sloping back, were known as the *Dinocephalia*, 'big heads'. They were possessed of incisor teeth, and one of them, *Lycosaurus*, the wolf lizard, had upper canine teeth like a lion's, whilst *Hyaenosuchus*, the 'hyaena crocodile', had ferocious canines. They probably preyed upon the slow-moving herbivorous anomodonts, 'odd-tooth', which in terms of numbers were the most successful of all the mammal-like reptiles.

Tusks are of great antiquity in the animal kingdom, for the anomodonts, although having a horny, turtle-like beak in place of teeth, also possessed a substantial pair of downward-pointing tusks in the upper jaw, circular in cross-section; these are thought to have been more for display than for grubbing up food. These were successful animals, and dicynodon, or the 'two dog-teeth' – the dicynodonts being the main herbivorous group – remained virtually unchanged for 20 million years. Rhachiocephalus, the 'ridge head', included giants with skulls 50 cm long but tuskless and narrow-snouted; in skull shape they were like the black rhinoceros, and were probably browsers. Aulacephalodon, the 'furrow-headed tooth', of which some reached a similar size, had, in contrast, a wider snout with a transverse cutting edge at the front and were probably grazers, forming the white rhinoceros equivalent. Lystrosaurus, the 'shovel lizard', had a worldwide distribution, and was probably the most successful single mammal-like reptile of all time; it is believed to have been an amphibious animal feeding in shallow water and behaving rather like a hippopotamus.

Kannemeyeria, its name relating to where it was first found, was, at about 3 metres long, one of the largest and best known; it was also a sort of reptilian hippo. It had a short skull with large tusks, but its eyes and nostrils were set on the top of its skull so that, like the hippo, it could float submerged with only its eyes and nostrils exposed – although as it did not have humans to fear what it was hiding from we do not know.

The early anomodonts were remarkable for their small size, 25–50 cm in length, compared with the dinocephalians, 2 metres and more. At that time South Africa was at high latitudes, so how did the dicynodonts survive the cold winters? Did they have a high metabolic rate so that they were in effect warm-blooded? Did they have some form of body insulation? Or did they hibernate during the winter? It is thought that they most probably had a high metabolic rate, their squat form with short tail and short limbs combining to reduce heat loss.

Then came the cynodonts, the last of the main therapsid groups to appear in the record, and the most closely related to mammals. They are called cynodonts, 'dog teeth', on account of a remarkable development of the cheek teeth behind the invariably prominent canines. Rather than simple pointed structures, the teeth had cusps or edges, and some had a grinding surface like those of mammals. The smallest cynodont was not much bigger than a rat, the largest the size of a wolf. But after flourishing for about 40 million years the therapsids had had their day and were replaced by the small almost-mammals: primitive crocodiles, primitive lizards, and primitive dinosaurs.

About 225 million years ago the first true mammals furtively appeared. Small, shrew-like creatures, these were the morganucodontids, 'Glamorgan teeth', named for where they were first found, in south Wales. The jaw of one of these rare animals (*Brancatherulum tendaguruense*) has been found in East Africa. The morganucodontids were accompanied by two other groups, the haramiyids, which petered out about 20 million years ago, and the kuehneotheriids, which produced a branch leading to present-day mammals. Possibly because of competition from the dinosaurs, these first mammals remained small, probably secretive, animals, until the extinction of the dinosaurs left the world open to them.

But from the first appearance of those mammals, about 225 million years ago, another 45 million years had passed before the dinosaurs flourished, relative latecomers to the vertebrate scene. Then East Africa really comes into its own with what was for a century Tanzania's best kept secret: the rich fossil deposits at Tendaguru near the coast. Tendaguru was a dinosaur graveyard, a veritable charnel house of dinosaur bones. As many as 50 animals have been found in one spot, suggesting they died in a drought at a dried-up waterhole. Most dinosaurs were no bigger than modern monitor lizards – but at Tendaguru limb bones have been found which are so huge they can only be lifted with a crane!

Some believed that for the giant dinosaurs to support their colossal weight they were semi-aquatic, their long neck – of which a single vertebra would measure over 1.2 metres in length – enabling them to live in deep water and keep their heads above the surface. But this view has now been challenged; it is thought that the water pressure would not allow them to breathe, and their limbs are more like those of creatures such as the elephant, which can carry a heavy weight on firm ground. The giant herbivorous dinosaurs are now seen as kinds of reptilian giraffe, the immensely long neck giving them access to a wide range of feeding levels. The great *Brachiosaurus brancai*, 'Branca's arm lizard', at one time called *Giraffatitani* or 'Titan's giraffe', was among the largest known of the dinosaurs. It was named after the German geologist von Branca, who had organized the Tendaguru excavations at the beginning of the 20th century. Then called *Brachiosaurus* after its American relative, because its forelegs were longer than its hind as in the giraffe, hence the original name of *Giraffatitani*, it is now considered a distinct species. Believed to have weighed some 23 to 37 tonnes (other estimates range from 15 to 78 tonnes) – the weight of five to ten adult bull elephants – this animal had a vast body with a long thin neck. Altogether it was some 18 to 24 metres in length, and could raise its head to 9 metres.

Another giant was the 20-metre-long *Tendaguria tanzaniensis*. The two lived alongside *Janenschia (Tornieria) africana*, about 18 metres long and standing 6 metres high at the shoulder, and the shorter *Dicraeosaurus*, the 'bifurcated lizard', almost 12 metres long and weighing from 3 to 40 tonnes depending upon how you estimate it. All of these dinosaurs also occurred in Malawi. *Barosaurus*, the 'heavy lizard', was also present at Tendaguru, a long-necked giant over 25 metres in length with an estimated weight of from 8 to 40 tonnes.

Among other types common at Tendaguru were whole herds of a relatively small form of the armoured dinosaur *Kentrosaurus aethiopicus*, the 'spiked African lizard'. This was the African equivalent of the American stegosaurus; at about 4.5 metres long and weighing anything from an estimated 1 to 4 tonnes, possibly because males and females differed in size, stegosaurus had an arched back adorned with erect paired plates surmounting it, changing to spines along its tail section. For years we were taught that the plates of stegosaurus were probably for heat dissipation, but it is clear that this would in fact have been armament to protect the otherwise vulnerable arched backbone, for in *Kentrosaurus*, which probably lived in a warmer climate than its American counterpart, half the adornment consists of spikes. Horrifying to look at, it was a harmless herbivore – unless you got in the way of its swinging spiked tail. Despite its size,

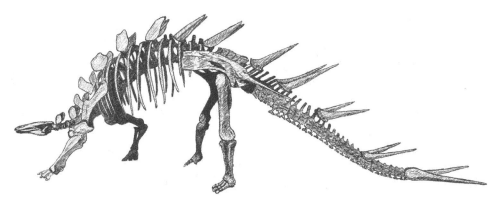

Kentrosaurus, a dinosaur from Tanzania.

its brain weighed a mere 56 grams, the smallest amongst the dinosaur assemblage, although it may have been supported possibly by an 835-gram lumbar brain, as was present in *barosaurus* and *dicraeosaurus*, believed to control the hindquarters; but the jury is out on the function of this organ.

Another abundant dinosaur at Tendaguru was the bipedal herbivorous ornithopod, bird-footed dinosaur, common elsewhere in the world, such as the small *dysalotosaurus* (*dryosaurus*) *lettowvorbecki* or 'Lettow-Vorbeck's uncatchable lizard' (named after the army commander in German East Africa in World War I, who was never caught), referred to as a tree-lizard, up to 4 metres in length and estimated to weigh about 104 kilos. Large numbers of this species have been found together, leading to the suggestion that they may have moved about in herds. Some bones showed a deformity believed to have been caused by a viral disease, which, if true, is the oldest viral infection known. Carnivorous types were represented by several forms of varying size; one of them, *Elaphrosaurus bambecki*, 'light-footed lizard', was a lightly built swift carnivore some 6 metres in length which ran on its hind legs. There were also the flying or gliding pterodactyls or pterosaurs, such as *Tendaguripterus recki*, 'Reck's winged tendaguru', with a 100-cm wingspan, named after Hans Reck, who discovered the Olduvai Gorge fossil deposits while hunting butterflies. Pterodactyls such as *Pterodactylus* and *Rhamphorhynchus* also occurred in East Africa, although their remains are rare. Some had a wingspan of 7.5 metres but, as usually found, most were much smaller than this.

How did this remarkable graveyard of giants come about at Tendaguru? It is a puzzle, to be sure, how so many apparently died together, especially *Kentrosaurus*, with over 50 found in one spot. Most likely they congregated at drying pools during a drought, as can be seen to be the fate of some elephants at waterholes today. Another possibility is that, slow-moving as the larger ones were, they would have been very susceptible to fire if the vegetation of the time was inflammable or became increasingly so as drier conditions prevailed. Some people think the bones simply accumulated over time. Most of the bones are very mixed up, indicating sorting by water action, leading to another suggestion that some dinosaurs became drowned by incoming tides when feeding in shallow lagoons. It is thought that in the age of these dinosaurs the Tendaguru region, now 80 kilometres inland, was a coastal area whose margin consisted of sand and mud flats through which a river branched, forming a delta with wide shallow lagoons isolated from the sea by barriers of sand. Periodic flooding would have swept river mud, silt, and dinosaur bones into the lagoons, whilst the coastline would have subsided at the same rate as the sediments were deposited, thus allowing sea sediments to be carried into the lagoons. Sharks' teeth and other marine fossils have been found at Tendaguru, as well as a brackish water fish, *Lepidotes tendagurensis*. It is believed that between about 127 and 157 million years ago earth movements caused the ocean to spread inland from the northeast, depositing sea sediments in shallow water on a continental shelf that became East Africa's present-day coastline. The Indian Ocean invaded and retreated three times, creating alternating sequences of marine and terrestrial sediments, thinning in the west to form the 140-metre-thick Tendaguru beds, at that time probably 3,400 kilometres south of the equator. The vegetation was apparently dominated by dry-adapted conifers, the second most frequent species being allied to the monkey puzzle tree, with some additional floral diversity.

But as the dinosaurs evolved, so too did some frightening carnivorous forms, although *Megalosaurus* or *Ceratosaurus*, the 'giant lizard' or 'horned lizard' – experts are undecided as to its true affinity – is known from only a single enormous tooth, but it was possibly a carnivore which walked on its hind legs, and bigger than an elephant. Most were smaller, like *Elaphrosaurus ornitholestes*, the 'bird-catcher', so named because it was at first thought to have seized bird-like creatures with its grasping-type hand.

Closely related to the dinosaurs are the crocodiles, abundant at that time. The least progressive of the ruling reptiles, they were to continue to survive with little change for a mind-boggling 65 million years after the last dinosaur became extinct, and are still common in parts of Africa today.

There has been much speculation as to why almost all this very successful group suddenly disappeared. This happened about 65 million years ago, when not only dinosaurs but 70 per cent of all animal life died out. A favoured theory is that this extinction was caused by a massive asteroid that struck Mexico at this time. However, a change to a drier climate seems more likely to have been the cause rather than a global cataclysmic event, although the asteroid strike could have caused climate change by creating vast dust clouds blocking out the sun. The giant dinosaurs would have required enormous quantities of lush vegetation to sustain them. Whatever the reason for the extinction, it was a boon for the mammals, the animals that suckle their young. Adapted to a drier environment, these now emerged from obscurity into a host of successful forms, egg-laying mammals being replaced by marsupials and placentals, those that partly rear the young inside the mother's body. The fossil record tells us that by the early Tertiary period, some 60 million years ago, placental mammals were becoming abundant in Africa.

Rodents, the gnawing mammals, and the hoofed mammals or ungulates, are found well developed in America at this time, but in the African fossil record many pages have not yet been found; not until the Eocene, 60 million years ago, do fossils reappear. Then we find an early forerunner of the elephant, a little pig-like animal called *Moeritherium* – a primitive dugong, ancestor of the marine dugong found today off African coasts – and several relatives of the hyrax, ranging in size up to as big as a lion.

Most spectacular of all this assembly of early African mammals was *Arsinoitherium*, named after the pharaoh Arsinoe I. The size of a rhino, it bore a huge pair of bone horns on the end of its snout, and a smaller pair above the eyes. This grotesque beast left no descendants, nor do we know from whence it came.

Primitive carnivores like *Hyaenodon* appeared in Africa 45 million years ago, along with primitive rodents and monkeys, and a hippo-like creature, the *Anthracothere*, 'coal beast', after the deposits in which it was first found. Other elephant types had evolved – forerunners of such mastodons as *Palaeomastodon* and *Phiomia*, 'animal of Fayum', already with tusks as big as those of a modern elephant's.

Ten million years later, in the Miocene, the fauna become increasingly modern in appearance, and East Africa has many remains from that epoch. Artiodactyls, 'even-toed mammals', were already the most important constituent; and the proboscideans, 'elephant-like animals', predated types such as *Deinotherium* and *Trilophodon*. The *deinothere*, 'terrible beast',

The tree hyrax rents the air at dawn and dusk with its piercing screams.

had tusks in its lower jaw which curved downwards and backwards. The bigger they grew, the slower it could chew; their weight must have given it constant jaw-ache. *Trilophodon* was also an odd sight, for it had a long face with a pair of slender upper tusks; whilst the lower jaw carried a pair of protruding, flattened, shovel-like teeth.

The elephants became great colonizers, reaching as far as North America, whilst their stay-at-home cousins, the hyraces, remained almost confined to Africa, only one form reaching Greece and one other Syria. Very conservative in their evolution, today there are only three types: the rock hyrax, the tree hyrax, and a less-common intermediate between the two. Rather like a large, coarse-haired guinea-pig (which originated in South America, not Guinea), the rock hyrax is the most widely distributed, living among crevices in rocks and occupying some of the most inaccessible places, its feet having a sucker-like action to allow it to grip smooth surfaces. The tree hyrax is a furry little animal that lives in holes in trees in the forest, and which rents the air at dawn and dusk with its piercing screams.

Suppose for a moment we could take a safari around Miocene East Africa. To the casual eye it would not look very different from today, with its hot dry plains and scattered thorn trees. Although many of the animals would be unfamiliar, we would probably be able to recognize most of them as related to present-day forms. In the woodlands we might see the earliest known bovid, *Eotragus*, 'dawn he-goat', duiker-like with a pair of small, upright horns. There was a deer-like creature, *Palaeomeryx africanus*, similar to the Asian musk deer, and a group of ruminants, some quite large, like the West African chevrotain. Ancestors of the duikers, and dik-dik, bushbuck, and hartebeests all seem to have been present, hartebeests being one of the most African of African animals. Many of the other ungulates – primitive deer and possibly the hippotragine, 'horse-eared', antelopes, such as the sable and roan – may have been invaders from the north.

We would see at least two sorts of rhinoceros, the same size as the black rhino but perhaps without horns. Several species of small pig scuttle about. If lucky we might see *Hyaenodon*, 'hyaena tooth', the primitive counterpart of the modern hyaena. A lingering survival of a group once numerous in other parts of the world, it has become extinct everywhere except in Africa. The place of the lion is taken by *Pseudaelurus*, the 'false sabre-tooth', so called because it was not a true cat, but had the sabre-tooth tiger's great canines.

In the water we might meet numerous hippopotamus-like creatures, the anthracothere *Hyoboops africanus*. Half the size of the modern hippo, they may well have been its ancestor. Gallery forests fringing the lakes and rivers were the home of small lemuroids, *Progalago minor*, similar to the modern bushbaby. Apes were plentiful, ranging in size from the little gibbon-like *Limnopithecus legetet* to *Proconsul major*, as big as a gorilla.

If we ventured onto the plains at night the animals would be even more familiar. Jumping hares, aardvarks, elephant shrews, numerous hedgehogs, tailless hares or picas (today found only in Europe and North America), and a kind of tenrec, representative of a shrew-like group now confined to Madagascar. We would find bats almost indistinguishable from those living today.

Africa has few remains from the next era, the Pliocene, to tell us how the animals were changing. But we can deduce that giraffe, hippo, black rhinoceros, and white rhinoceros, as well as hyaena, must have appeared on the scene. This comparatively sudden appearance of

Encephalartos, one of the most primitive of living plants, an ancient survival in Tanzania.

many types has led to the suggestion that they were immigrants from Asia. For example, the earliest known true hippos appear in the Lower Pliocene of India, and the fact that that hippo once lived in London's Trafalgar Square shows how mammals could radiate. But conditions for fossilization may just not have been good enough in Africa at that time to provide us with the missing links.

Fossils are not lacking for the true age of mammals, the Pleistocene era, which as we have seen began about 2.5 million years ago. In Africa alone at least 130 now extinct species appeared, in addition to most of those now living, but in general the continent still looked much the same as it does today. During the frequent wet periods there was more forest, but it was not very different in appearance from now; the days of the rich carboniferous forests with their galaxy of fleshy palms and ferns are 350 million years behind us. Only a few rare traces remain, such as *Encephalartos*, 'bread within the head', still existing in Uganda and Tanzania and other parts of Africa, an ancient cycad related to the conifers, one of the most primitive of living plants. Known as the bread tree, its scientific name refers to its starchy fruit.

During the dry periods conditions like those we find today in northern Kenya were widespread, and all the shallower lakes we know of were probably dry. This would have caused important redistributions of fish populations, but would have had less effect upon the mammals.

Most of our knowledge of the Pleistocene comes from the rich finds of the famous Olduvai Gorge of Tanzania, where over 100 different species of animals have been unearthed. It became world famous for the discovery of Nutcracker Man, *Zinjanthropus boisei*, now *Paranthropus*, or 'past man', once claimed to be the earliest known human which was not an ape; in other words, an ape that used tools it had made itself. Now, however, the earliest human is believed to date from 2.8 million years ago in Ethiopia, but as its identity is based only upon a fragment of jaw we cannot tell much about this ancestor of ours.

Let us take another safari, this time into a Pleistocene day. I think we would find it more exciting than our Miocene trip, as there would be many strange-looking animals among the rich fauna. The deinothere survived well into the middle of this era, and there was the nightmarish chalicothere, *Metaschitzotherium* (*Phyllotillon*), a great sloth-like creature with grasping claws instead of hooves, justifying its scientific name of 'unreal great beast'. Its forelegs were longer than its hind, and it probably used its claws for pulling down branches. On the plains we would find its more familiar relatives, the Burchell's and Grevy's zebras, as well as a little three-toed horse, *Stylohipparion*. This dwarf horse survived here long after becoming extinct in its original home range of Eurasia and North America. Another strange co-existence was the short-necked giraffid, *Sivatherium*, 'Shiva's beast', after its counterpart first found in India, and once known as *Libytherium*, the 'African wild beast', with massive antlers in contrast to the short stubs serving the present-day giraffe it browsed side by side with.

The Lower Pleistocene saw the appearance of the first true elephants, living together with mastodons like *Anancus*, which was about 2.4 metres tall and had long, straight tusks. Then there were the stegodons, the first to show the characteristic tooth structure of true elephants. Instead of separate teeth all in the jaw at once, they had a single giant molar. When worn out, this was replaced by another, and so on until a complement of six in each jaw was exhausted, just as in the modern elephant. This meant that the stegodons' ability to grind their food would last some six times longer, prolonging the animal's life without having an enormous length of jaw which would have required increased muscles to bear its weight and so require an even greater food supply.

Mammoths, the best known of all fossil proboscideans – animals with trunks – were here also. They looked much like living elephants, but bore very long tusks that curved inwards at their tips. It has been suggested this was for use as a snowplough when searching for food. Not of much use to them in the tropics! As all tusks grow in a spiral, they would, if they grew for long enough, turn inward at their tips without this being of any functional use.

By the middle of the Pleistocene all of these elephants had disappeared and were replaced by the straight-tusked elephant, *Palaeoloxodon antiquus*. This animal was 4.2 metres high at the shoulder and carried tusks 3.3 metres in length, the biggest elephant ever known.

It was bigness that made the next period, the Middle Pleistocene, about a million years ago, the most exciting. It was another age of giants after the dinosaurs. There was the monstrous 'sheep', *Pelorovis*, the size of a rhino and with great down-curving horns with a span of 1.8 metres. Now believed to be a buffalo, had it been a sheep it would have been the only one ever found south of the Sahara. Another giant buffalo, *Bularchus*, with similar great horns, was also present. There was a giant kudu, bigger than its modern counterpart, among other giant antelopes. *Giraffa jumae* was a giraffe even bigger than the sivathere (more about this at the end of Chapter 3). There were great pigs; the tusks of one, *Afrochoerus*, were four times the length of those of the living warthog, and its skull was bigger than a rhino's. Yet this surprising creature had cheek teeth smaller than those of our living giant forest hog. Little wonder *Afrochoerus* could not survive when conditions became drier, for it would not have been able to chew enough food; its teeth would have worn out too quickly. Great apes in the shape of a giant baboon, *Simopithecus oswaldi*, a frightening giant sabre-toothed cat, *Dinofelis*, and an ostrich, *Struthio oldowayi* – twice the height of the living 2.4-metre-tall bird – added to this bizarre assembly.

Of course there were plenty of what would be to us normal-looking animals, the ones able to survive when conditions became unfavourable for large size. Pigs of various kinds were among the most common. All living antelopes were probably present, with many more gazelles than exist today. There was also a carnivore that seems to have been more closely allied to the tiger than to the lion, arriving late on the scene.

Now taking the place of the anthracotheres were several kinds of hippo, from the 90 cm high *Hippopotamus imaguncula* to the great pop-eyed hippo, *Hippopotamus gorgops*, larger than its living relative. Its eyes were very high on the head, suggesting an extremely wary habit; but again, what might have preyed upon it in the water we do not know.

These awe-inspiring giants of the Middle Pleistocene have created much speculation as to what caused such exuberant development. But there is nothing strange about giantism in evolution: animal life seems to develop as many and as big forms as possible until natural selection comes along and scythes them down to more realistic shapes and sizes. We saw giantism among the reptiles, and amongst the mammals it was not peculiar to Africa but occurred throughout the world. Europe produced the Irish elk, *Megaceros*, a giant deer. Russia produced an even bigger ostrich than Africa did, and Australia produced giant kangaroos and a wombat the size of a rhino, whilst Madagascar produced lemurs with skulls over a foot long, and the famous elephant birds, *Aepyornis*, which laid 2-gallon eggs.

Africa's giants appear suddenly, and just as suddenly disappear. A period of mammalian effusiveness, the Pleistocene was equally a period of catastrophic extinction. In one arid interval of the Lower Pleistocene at Olduvai, 60 per cent of the fauna became extinct. Later, 40 per cent of the remainder disappeared, and then 40 per cent again. Thus by the Upper Pleistocene, about a third of a million years ago, almost all of the fauna were modern. But if we visited Olduvai, then we would still have a few surprises, finding animals that today are very restricted in range: the mountain nyala, confined to a small part of Ethiopia, and the hunter's antelope, now found in only a small area of Kenya. Even the okapi, unchanged since the Miocene, can be found at Olduvai, and the area contains a plentiful array of the less common species in East Africa today: greater and lesser kudu, sable, roan, eland, oryx, white rhino, and others. At that time chimpanzees occurred around Kenya's Lake Naivasha, 640 kilometres east of their present range.

A visit to a game park today has been referred to as like taking a peep at a Pleistocene day. And so it is – but a very poor one. Casual visitors may well be impressed by the number and diversity of the animals they see, but had they visited the same place in the Pleistocene and seen only what they see today, they would soon have demanded their money back!

3

Evolution in action

The great age of mammals awaits humanity's *coup de grâce*. But even as it does so, evolution, slowly but defiantly, still takes place. Most animals are changing continually. A population suddenly severed by a river may evolve into two separate forms. Likewise a population separated in time by several thousand years from its ancestors will comprise quite different-looking descendants. There are of course exceptions; a few sluggards of nature like the coelacanth, the marine fish of the East African coast that has remained unchanged for 300 million years, and then there is the lungfish of Africa, which also occurred 300 million years ago, and which has only four known species despite the time it has had to evolve further.

If we look at the changes too closely we find ourselves in quite a muddle should we try to pigeonhole animals into separate groups, for most of the changes, in space or in time, have connecting links. So we can either lump all of our forms together, ignoring the extreme differences, or, as is more commonly done, divide them into arbitrary groups.

At the beginning of the 20th century, when big game hunting was in its heyday, a hunter's greatest ambition was not to shoot the animal with the biggest pair of horns or tusks, but to have a new species named after him (it would always have been a him). As a result, if an animal showed the slightest difference from the one already on record, the skin was hurried back to a museum where it was solemnly pronounced to be a new species or sub-species. For a suitable sum it could even bear the hunter's name. No account was taken of the animal's sex, age, or individual variation. Some giraffe subspecies or races were described simply from a fragment of skin or a single skull. It is hardly surprising to learn that 16 races of giraffe were described, of which genetics today show that from an original base in East Africa 6 to 11 species evolved, possibly 9. This is nothing compared to the waterbuck with 37 races, or the hartebeest with 36. Even the lion had 19 races described.

Races are usually described based upon somewhat subtle variations in coat colour and pattern, horn shape and size, body size, etc., with more fundamental differences giving them species status. But many of these differences are not obvious at first sight. Few visitors to Kenya's

[Clockwise from above]

Lungfish taking air. An ancient relic.

Typical Grant's gazelle.

Mixed forest and Cape buffalo
types in western Uganda.

Tsavo National Park would realize the difference between the Peter's gazelle they can see there and the typical Grant's gazelle. Peter's is simply a race distinguished by the buck's short, nearly straight, horns, and its white rump patch divided into two, compared with the more substantial curved horns of the typical Grant's gazelle and its undivided white rump patch.

An area where the animals show considerable variability is that separating the typically West African fauna of the Congo Rainforest from the East African fauna of the open savannahs. This zone is formed by the western Rift Valley and is typified by the Queen Elizabeth Park in Uganda. In 5 square kilometres here I found three quite different-looking buck waterbuck; each on its appearance alone would have qualified as a 'race'. Buffalo, being on the edge of the tropical forest, show all shades of colour and all shapes of horn and body size in a single herd. Their colour may range from completely rufous, like the red forest buffalo of the Congo, to the jet black of the big Cape buffalo of the open plains. And their horns vary too, from the small weapons of the forest buffalo to the sweeping, massive armament borne by the Cape buffalo.

Forest elephants in their forest habitat.

Not quite so obvious, but just as common here, are the elephant varieties. These show every form from the almost typical Congo Forest elephant – small, and with long, thin, downward-pointing tusks and rounded ears – to the bush elephant – much larger, with angular ears and thicker, upward-curving tusks.

These zones of mixed forms tend to be narrow. The distinct forms on either side of the zone in question may gain some particular advantage from their racial traits, meaning that each is at a disadvantage in the other's habitat; in other words, the red forest buffalo may not be able to live out on the hot, dry plains, and the black Cape buffalo may not be able to live in the humid forest. Thus the two populations cannot mix. But in the transitional zone, where there is a little of both worlds, they do mix, although the resultant forms are unlikely to have an advantage in either habitat; neither can become more numerous than the other, as there is nothing to favour it. Thus a balance of mixed forms is obtained. Unless conditions change to favour them they represent an evolutionary cul-de-sac.

The most obvious way in which variation might arise is by geographical isolation through the formation of deserts, rivers, mountains, or forests severing a population into two or more units. The animals so isolated then tend to diverge in character. A good example is the black-and-white colobus monkey, easily distinguished from all other monkeys by not possessing a thumb. A lover of tall forest, it has separated into five species and some sixteen subspecies. Mount Kenya has its own species, as has Mount Kilimanjaro. In the lowland forest, between the Ruwenzori Mountains and the River Congo, are two species that, once separated, have now come together again and are found living side by side, yet do not interbreed.

Some animal species that have diverged from one another have, however, met again before separation is complete to the extent of not being able to interbreed. One example is the waterbuck: a fine antelope, the ruff on the buck's shaggy bearded throat gives such an air of grandeur to its noble carriage with head held high. Two races are usually recognized, the common waterbuck or *Ellipsiprymnus*, which only occurs east of the eastern Rift Valley; and the defassa waterbuck, much more widely distributed to the west of the Valley. The first takes its scientific name, *Ellipsiprymnus*, from the white ellipse around its buttocks, looking 'as if it had sat on a newly-painted lavatory seat', and the other from its Ethiopian name, *defassa*, having a white blaze on its rump. In areas where both types are found, as in the Nairobi Park of Kenya, zones occur where animals showing all degrees of intermediate rump pattern exist, although

The common or *ellipsiprymnus* waterbuck.

[Left] The defassa waterbuck.

[Below] The common or Masai giraffe has a vine-leaf pattern, fawn in colour on an off-white background.

the coat colouring and appearance is more like that of the common. These are crosses between the two extremes, although as we saw elsewhere, the zones of mixing remain small.

As with waterbuck, so are there meeting zones of the reticulated and the common, or Masai, giraffe. The reticulated giraffe, confined to northern Kenya and southern Somalia, is the most distinctive of all giraffes. It has beautiful angular liver-red patches on a very white network. The Masai giraffe, which occurs throughout much of Kenya and Tanzania, has fawn patches with dissected edges – the vine-leaf pattern – on an off-white background. Never have I seen a true reticulated giraffe mixed up with Masai giraffes or vice versa, although it is said to occur in meeting zones. What one does see where giraffes are very variable in pattern, particularly in the Nairobi Park, are giraffes with liver-red patches on a white background, but the patches have dissected outlines. Or giraffes with angular patches, but the colouring is fawn on an off-white background. This has led observers to claim they have seen crosses between the two types of giraffe, although there are no reticulated giraffes within many kilometres of Nairobi Park. Giraffes cross freely in zoos, but there is no information as to how successful this is. How many of the offspring survive compared with those of normal pairings? Can they reproduce themselves efficiently? Or does indiscriminate crossing lead to dwindling captive populations whose causes are ascribed elsewhere?

Efficient reproduction, as against casual crosses, is a fair sign of lack of distinction between populations, the criterion for what constituted a species being whether or not two animals could breed together and produce offspring that could breed in turn.

Contrary to expectation, in spite of their mobility birds are very stick-in-the-mud creatures, extremely prone to variation by isolation. If climatic change does not force them to move, then populations will stay in one spot for so long that they can form sub-species. There is a thrush on Mount Kilimanjaro, the Taita Hills of Kenya, and the North Pare Mountains of Tanzania, which has evolved from an original stock into sub-species on mountains that are in sight of one another. The same is true of a francolin, a partridge-like bird on Mount Kenya and the Aberdare mountains of Kenya, whose common relative of the plains, the red-legged francolin, heralds the dawn with its noisy call.

Birds of the mountain forests differ from those of the lowland forests, and those of the lowland forests differ from those of the open plains. In mammals, however, there are no such clear-cut distinctions. Certain mammals are adapted to life either in the forest or on the plains,

A red-legged francolin, herald of the African morning.

but this is about as far as it goes. Where mountain races occur they are generally closely related to widespread lowland forms; for example, both the shaggy-coated Mount Kenya hyrax and the Ruwenzori golden cat have similar lowland relations.

Evolution in an isolated location is a speeded-up process of the evolution that takes place in a continuous population spread over a large area. The pattern of inheritance is so complex that it does not reproduce itself perfectly every time, so at the extremes of a range animals may look quite different from one another. Rather like the game of Chinese whispers. Once the changes have been made, the extremes remain different; the pattern cannot breed back along the line but gets lost on the way, just as the original pattern did when moving in the opposite direction. When the two extremes have become sufficiently distinct from each other they can no longer interbreed; then they are separate species and the transfer of inherited characters between them ceases. All those left in between, which may not look the same but can still interbreed, are known as subspecies or races.

That was the theory; but in practice two animals may have looked so different that although they could interbreed we still preferred to call them different species. But now the study of animal genes has overthrown that rule of thumb, and a species is now defined as an animal with a distinct number of chromosomes, the organs within a cell that hold the genes, despite the animal's outward appearance. This has thrown up new species that were not apparent before, as in the case of crocodiles or elephants. The animals may have looked similar to one another, but now their chromosome complements have shown them to be distinct species.

So we see that distinctions between species are not very clear-cut. Without counting chromosomes we are in some doubt as to whether different-looking forms are in fact different species, or in some cases even different genera. This is because mammals in particular tend to be very ubiquitous. There are few cases of them developing in isolation through choice; mostly, if that occurs at all, it is only temporary. It comes as a surprise therefore when we look at some of the fishes of the African lakes to find that speciation has literally run riot.

Nobody knows quite how many different species of fish exist, or did exist, in Lakes Tanganyika, Victoria, and Malawi; but each lake appears to have, or did have, about 280, 350 and 600, species of fish respectively, each of which is found nowhere else! But when in the 1950s Nile perch were introduced to Lake Victoria its species were reduced by about a half. These endemics, as they are called, are almost all cichlids, the aquarist's well-known mouth-breeders, which shelter the newly-hatched young in the mouth when danger threatens. Perch-like in appearance, these fishes are widespread in Africa, ranging in size from 2–5 cm in length to over 30 cm. The most common genus is *Haplochromis*. They can be very pretty; the males, in scarlet and emerald breeding dress with black ventral fins, equal the best of tropical fishes for colour display. But as soon as you take them from the water their colours fade.

But how could so many species – species, mark you, not sub-species – have evolved together like this? Are fish so conservative in their movements that there is virtually no interchange within these lakes, causing hundreds of little pockets each to evolve separately? This seems most unlikely. It has been suggested that past fluctuations in lake depths, isolating a population in a swamp here, another there, and so on through their history, have been responsible for creating this multitude of species.

A colourful cichlid fish from the Akagera River, Rwanda.

The speciation created different feeding habits. Some became strictly shallow-water bottom feeders, others insectivorous, and others predacious. Such tremendous competition has led to somewhat bizarre speciation. Most extraordinary is that shown by two related *Corematodus* species in Lake Malawi. To pass unnoticed they mimic the colour pattern of a shoaling plankton feeder, *Oreochromis*. When they are thus insinuated into the shoal, their diet comprises scales nibbled off the tails of their unsuspecting hosts!

We cannot leave the subject of evolution without mentioning the giraffe, used for generations as a simple example of how evolution works in many popular accounts, but now more used as a stick to beat Darwin with by those who do not accept the idea of evolution by natural selection (that is, a struggle to succeed in nature, those with small advantages outdoing those without them). The giraffe became a pivotal species in the controversy surrounding the mechanism of evolution when in 1809 the French scientist Lamarck noted:

> It is interesting to observe the result of habit in the peculiar shape and size of the giraffe (Camelo-pardalis): this animal, the largest of the mammals, is … obliged to browse on the leaves of trees and to make constant efforts to reach them. From this habit long maintained in all its race, it has resulted that the animal's forelegs have become longer than its hind legs, and that its neck is lengthened to such a degree that the giraffe, without standing on its hind legs, attains a height of six metres.

Twenty years passed before he came under attack from the leading French naturalist Baron Cuvier, an attack launching a controversy which still rumbles on today, basically that an animal could not evolve according to its 'needs' or 'desires', as Lamarck was interpreted. So how did the giraffe get its long neck? One theory was that those with longer necks than usual had an advantage when food was scarce, thus outliving those with shorter necks. Another that it was not food at all which was the driving force, but the ability to use the tall neck as a watch-tower to spot predators. It was not until 1872, in his sixth edition of his *Origin of Species*, that Charles Darwin joined the debate: 'So under nature with the nascent giraffe, the individuals which were the highest browsers and were able during dearths to reach even an inch or two above the others, will often have been preserved.' These would, he wrote, have bred to produce an animal just as tall, and when the next dearth came along the same process would operate, producing even taller animals, ending with, 'it seems to me almost certain that an ordinary hoofed quadruped might be converted into a giraffe'.

One contemporary dismissed Darwin's explanation on the grounds that the cow giraffe is about 0.6 metres shorter than the bull, and so if natural selection had anything to do with it only the bulls would be selected for survival. The young would likewise tend to be eliminated. A more recent proposal was that the long forelegs were the important feature, developed for speed to escape lions, and having long legs the giraffe would have to have a long neck to be able to drink. Another, that its long shape could have evolved for heat dissipation to withstand intense solar radiation, whilst at the same time conferring all the advantages which large size endowed. But whilst some modifications to the feeding competition theory have been attempted, neither predator avoidance nor long shape for heat loss have gained subsequent support.

Much feeding by giraffes is at relatively low levels, craning the neck downwards, principally upon low bushes in the dry season and turning to tall acacia trees in the wet season, when leaves are rich and plentiful. But some people argue that feeding habits are not correlated with an advantageous neck length, and that although giraffes may have spent more time feeding at low level than at high, apart from the fact that to be significant this must be related to availability of high as opposed to low shoots, this does not negate the fact that the animal with a long neck has an advantage in that it can feed at high levels if there is a scarcity of food at low ones. But this argument does not take account of the fact that evolutionary pressures were most likely to operate in prolonged periods of pronounced aridity which extended over thousands of years (not in annual alternating wet and dry seasons), and the competitive conditions under which the giraffe achieved its present form (not its current competitive relationships). Dismissing the 'watchtower' hypothesis, studies in South Africa showed twice as many bull as cow giraffes taken by lions, but did show a capture success with giraffes over and above that of other large species. But in the Kruger National Park giraffes, where present, generally constituted about 2.0 per cent of the large mammal fauna, but represented less than 2.0 per cent of all kills, the main predator being lion.

The latest theory argues for sexual selection based on the neck, elongation of the neck reflecting selective advantage in sparring, the length of the neck arising from its use as a weapon in the bull used for fighting other bulls; as it is the large-necked bulls who gain access to the cows who are ready to pair, this drives the neck ever longer. This does not obviously explain the long neck of the cow, but in fact because sexual selection drove bull necks ever larger, cow necks followed, as they cannot be genetically uncoupled from increases in body size. Just as many doe antelope carry horns, so the cow giraffe has small ossicones, although in fighting she does not use her head; instead, as detailed later on, she kicks. It has been suggested that the long neck in the cow disguises the gender of bull offspring, in that the similarity between cows and bulls allows the bull offspring to develop to independence without adult bull attacks.

So these theories bring us no nearer to a convincing explanation – but all the arguments relate to the giraffe evolving *upward*, whereas the giraffe has all the appearance of a slimmed-down sivathere-like animal.

The sivathere had its origins in India alongside the giraffe; *Sivatherium giganteum* was a large, apparently cumbersome, stocky animal the size of an elephant, with huge, palmate, antler-like horns. But as this head armament became bigger and bigger, giving the owner a temporary advantage in protecting itself or competing with its rivals, so it imposed increasing strains. Massive neck muscles would have been required, with a shortening of the body to give more efficient leverage, and the increase in size meant an increase in food until the limits of sustainability of large body size would have been reached.

But if the animal lost its head armament, with one bound it would have been free. There would be no need for the massive neck muscles, neither would it need pillar-like legs to support its great weight; instead it could rely upon speed to escape its enemies, using thinned-down stilt-like legs, lengthened to increase its stride. Needing some armament for battling rivals, shortened bony knobs sufficed. In which case the giraffe never had to evolve upward; it could have derived from a thinned-down sivathere-like animal.

But that's just another theory.

Giraffe evolution. (Image: d'Ache, Caran. n.d. (c. 1900). Album Caran d'Ache. album deuxième. Paris: Librairie Plon. p. 30.)

4

Animal colours

Lacking the vibrant colours shown by birds and fishes, mammals nevertheless display an attractive range of colours in many different patterns. Using just two pigments, black eumelanin, and light brown to yellow phaeomelanin – or in their absence, white – almost all of the complex colours of hair-covered mammals are produced.

Monkeys, like the cheeky vervet, add bright red and blue by combinations of blood and skin, and the hippo perspires a red pigment when it leaves the water that, while not a skin colouring, acts as a kind of sun-tan lotion, preventing its skin from becoming sunburnt.

Birds make use of more pigments and use them in fewer ways, but it is among the reptiles that most pigments are used and the most varied colours produced. The best-known example of what the reptiles can do, the chameleon, has four layers in its skin: a background layer of black or brown, a white reflecting layer, a blue reflecting layer, and a final yellow pigmented layer. The yellow pigment is enclosed in long, branching cells that extend among the other layers. If a chameleon wants to look yellow, all it has to do is to expand these cells. To become green it shrinks them a little. This lets reflected blue light pass through, mixing with the yellow to give green. When one male chameleon meets another male chameleon he becomes black with rage. This is because the bottom melanin layer spreads up over the yellow.

The little African reed or tree frogs, *Hyperoliidae*, use an almost identical method, but may have red instead of yellow pigment. These frogs are interesting as although they are exactly like a South American counterpart they evolved from quite separate origins, an example of parallel evolution. The African species mostly inhabit grassland, and shrubs near water, although there is one forest species that has such large webbed feet it can glide from tree to tree. Their preferred food is winged insects such as flying ants. Most active at dusk, they do not feed during the day, remaining in characteristic attitude tightly pressed to a stem or leaf. Possessing a wide range of colours, some are capable of rapid colour changes, whereas others merely go rather pale on light backgrounds. With three kinds of pigment cells – black or brown; yellow or red; and white – they produce green by absorbing all colours except blue, reflecting this back off the

African reed frog.

white and filtering it through the yellow. The function of the colouration in the more decorative ones is probably just as much for camouflage as it is in the drabber species. I discovered that the best way to find reed frogs was to drive slowly through wet grass and they would hop onto the vehicle.

In the past animal colours never failed to excite many lively arguments due to a liberal use of the term 'protective colouration'. As Theodore Roosevelt, the naturalist-president of the United States, put it:

> In South America concealing colouration plays no more part in the lives of the
> adult deer, the tamandua, the tapir, the peccary, the jaguar, and the puma, than
> it plays in Africa in the lives of such animals as the zebra, the sable antelope, the
> wildebeest, the lion and the hunting dog.

The fault lay in looking for a *single* explanation. A fellow American naturalist, Abbott Thayer, went so far as to paint a picture of pink flamingos in a red sunset, to show how well camouflaged they were against the right background. Roosevelt retorted in effect that Thayer might as well have painted a raven in a coal-scuttle!

> The raven's coloration is of course concealing if it is put into a coal scuttle; and
> if chalk is added to the contents of the coal scuttle, than a magpie's coloration
> might also become concealing under the same circumstances.

But the causes of an animal's colouration vary from animal to animal, just as the animals' lives vary. So we must look for more than one factor to explain it.

Sir Percy Fitzpatrick, with his long experience of hunting in the South African bush in the 19th century, thought that among the larger animals it worked through two things: absolute

Flamingos at dawn on Lake Nakuru, Kenya.

stillness, and breaking up the colour. He considered that no wild animal, except those protected by distance and open country, will stand against a background of light or uniform colour, nor as a rule allow its own shape to form an unbroken patch against the background. The contrasting black and white stripes of the zebra in the bush enable it to hide at will:

> I have seen a wildebeest effectually hidden by a single blighted branch; a
> koodoo bull, by a few twisty sticks; a crouching lion, by a wisp of feathery grass
> no higher than one's knee, no bigger than a vase of flowers!

In fact, although an animal's dress may be for camouflage, it can equally well be for advertising the owner's presence, warning others to keep away. It may be for social recognition, or sexual attraction. It may be physiological, a purely incidental by-product of the animal's body; or even evolved to assist the body's workings in some way. Or a combination of two or more of these. In addition, an animal's dress may have evolved in its past history for reasons no longer important. This could explain the colour of the hunting dog, whose blotchy colouration perhaps once helped it to hunt singly by stealth instead of openly in packs as it does today.

If an animal remains motionless when danger threatens, like the African hare that crouches immobile until you almost tread upon it, this is usually a sign that it is using its dress for concealment: 'cryptic colouration'. One day I flushed a hare on almost bare, burnt, ground. As it raced away a hawk swooped on it but missed. Instantly the hare froze, completely in the open, and the hawk circled at a loss, quite unable to spot the motionless form. When the hawk had risen a little the hare raced for a bush and hid itself. By this time the hawk was joined by another, and both perched in the bush to wait for the hare to re-appear, which was hardly playing the game!

[Clockwise from top left]

Greater kudu bull in Botswana.

The African hare relies on its colouration and immobility to escape detection.

Newborn Thomson's gazelle relying on its protective colouration to escape detection.

Many newborn antelopes have neutral colours, drab light browns almost indistinguishable from dry vegetation. If the baby is unable to run fast at birth, and the mother unable to defend it against the larger predators, she tries to divert danger from her offspring by leaving it alone. Pressed tightly against the ground, the young eliminates all shadows and blends perfectly with its background. Its lack of scent means the predator cannot find it by smell. It is at this stage that people sometimes come across these youngsters and pick them up as 'abandoned', when of course they are not.

But of what use, to large animals like wildebeest or hartebeest, is their drab colouring? They do not try to hide themselves when danger threatens. We could ask the same of the zebra's enigmatic stripes. To us they produce an optical illusion, making the zebra difficult to see clearly at a distance. But is this of any real advantage to the zebra? Perhaps the stripes are of advantage at dusk, or at dawn, on moonless nights, or perhaps on moonlit nights? Daytime is a period of comparative inactivity for carnivores, so perhaps we should think about what animal colours will look like at night, when everything is seen by most, if not all, animals, in shades of grey. Many mammals have dichromatic vision (that is, they see blue, yellow, black, white, and shades of grey), and at night they see in black, white and grey, as we humans do. But look at an ungulate's eye; there is no visible 'white', and the iris can dilate to the edge of the eyelid, an indication of its ability, better than ours, to pick up low-intensity light.

The zebra's striped football jersey may be a step in evolution from an ancestral spotted forest form. This transition is seen in carnivores, from the spots of the forest-dwelling leopard to stripes in the Asiatic tiger, and to nothing at all in the lion. The now extinct quagga zebra of South Africa had lost nearly all of its stripes (or never possessed any), perhaps associated with its life in the open, and representing the end-point of a series. Like the carnivores, which end with the lion of the open plains.

The carnivores' spotted pattern is regarded as primitive because it is usually present in the young, even if it is absent in the adult. The young of carnivores are born blind and helpless, and must be hidden away and guarded by the parents. There is no necessity therefore for their colour to be adaptive. As it grows up the lion tends to lose its spots, but some individuals retain well-defined spots on the belly almost throughout life. The leopard keeps them because of its life in the trees and bush, where its pattern mingles admirably with the flecks of dappled sunlight. The spotted pattern of the cheetah may be of advantage in allowing it to get within striking distance of its prey, but it often approaches its prey openly. Its cubs are unique in having a mantle of long bluish-grey hair that reaches from the neck along the length of the back, and dark legs and underside, the latter looking like shadow under the light upper area which, combined, possibly helps to conceal the cubs in long grass, for cheetah cubs, unlike those of other carnivores, are not born in lairs but in tall grass and undergrowth. The cubs lose the mantle at about four months old, leaving just a ruff of longer hair on the shoulders and the back of the neck.

Apart from merely acting as camouflage, it has been suggested that patterns may be protective in other ways by making use of optical effects. Thus disruptive patterning distracts attention from the object as a whole and focuses it on one particular point. An example of this might be the broad black flank band of the Thomson's gazelle. The value of this is suggested to lie in the split-second advantage this may give by distracting a predator's gaze, so the hunted has a chance to spot the hunter before it itself is perceived. Instant avoidance reaction is far more important to a hunted animal than is maintained speed. Animals do not stop to think – they react.

But in my experience of watching predators in Africa, they study the prey most carefully beforehand for what seems an interminable length of time. Lions stare fixedly at their prey when beginning a stalk, very rarely snatching at something they come across by chance. This is left to scavengers like the hyaena. In the Grant's gazelle, a close relative of the Tommy, the flank band is missing in the buck but present in the doe, suggesting it is more of a species' recognition signal than a disruptive pattern.

The eye of the oryx is surrounded by a dark stripe, said to camouflage the eye so that a watching lion cannot determine if the oryx is looking at it. Unlikely, I think, though, as the attitude of the head would tell the lion more than movements of the eyeball.

Lions do hunt by sight. This is why, in common with those of other large carnivores, the lion's eyes are directed forwards, giving them good binocular vision so they can judge distances accurately. The region of the brain associated with smell is reduced in the lion compared to

[From top]

The zebra's pattern offers no protection.

Lion families showing the spotted pattern of the cubs.

Thomson's gazelle with its distinctive black flank stripe.

that of the herbivores. It is a popular belief that when darkness falls in Africa the land becomes alive with hunting animals, for lions often do hunt at night. Probably they do this because it is cooler to do so, but as we have seen, it is also possible that an animal's colour operates more as a camouflage at night than it would seem to do during the day.

I spent many nights out in the Queen Elizabeth Park in Uganda watching waterbuck, and found the nights to be very quiet; it was the only time that a buck waterbuck would go to sleep – but not for longer than four minutes at a time!

An optical principle employed is counter-shading. This is seen in many species that have a white belly. The white reduces the intensity of the shadow, giving the animal a more uniform appearance; but it may be of more importance physiologically, to deflect heat reflected from the ground away from the animal's belly.

There is one example in which this is reversed: the ratel or honeybadger. Although it is much like the European badger in general appearance, the ratel has a light grey back and black lower parts. Mainly nocturnal, it seems admirably camouflaged in the moonlight when so much is in deep shadow.

Unlike the chameleon, most mammals cannot change their colour except over a period of time, such as from winter to summer. (The exception is humans, who can make rapid social signals by blushing.) So in terms of camouflage, a mammal's colour must always be a compromise, as most mammals move about a great deal. But they can resort to tricks, using two methods at once: self-advertisement and concealment. The bushbuck of western Uganda is a pretty antelope. It has white spots and stripes on its rufous coat, and a large fluffy, powder-puff tail, white on the underside. When it runs for cover it holds its tail in the air, just like a rabbit, a white flag for all to see. Then as it takes a nosedive into a bush it abruptly folds its tail down, and creeps away in the thicket. The sudden disappearance of the white signal confuses the eye. You, or the predator, remain staring at the spot where you last saw it.

While I was crouching silently among the rocks on a kopje one day, waiting to photograph a klipspringer, an animal that blends well into its habitat, a leopard suddenly appeared, picking its way along among the rocks. It wasn't hunting, for its tail was held upright and its white underside tuft at the tip waved ridiculously like a flag as it walked. Was it a signal perhaps to cubs following behind? In which case I was lucky it did not see me, as leopards are known for their ferocious defence of their young. Or was it simply signalling that it was not hunting? It was certainly intended to advertise the owner's presence.

Total advertisement, or warning colouration, is usually restricted to black-and-white signals, and is only carried by animals that can be very unpleasant if their warning goes unheeded, although this does not apply to the zebra, whose flesh is favoured by all carnivores. The best-known example is the skunk, which has its African counterpart in the zorilla, an almost identical-looking animal. If attacked, the zorilla merely lifts its tail and squirts the attacker with an evil-smelling oily liquid. So objectionable is the smell that the attacker – usually a domestic dog that then has to spend several days shut outside, to add to its misery – never forgets the colour pattern of the zorilla.

One might expect poisonous snakes to be warningly coloured, but very few are. Most are protectively coloured. This apparent anomaly is because their poison is primarily for capturing prey, which they hunt by stealth. However deadly they may be, most poisonous snakes try to

[Clockwise from top left]

Lions hunt by night as well as by day.

The ratel or honey badger.

A bushbuck. It only reveals its white
tail underside when it runs away.

escape rather than bite a large animal that they cannot eat. Unfortunately a snake like the puff-adder is so sluggish, and so cleverly camouflaged, that it is often trodden on by mistake and sometimes gives a fatal bite in return. I once disturbed a puff-adder in entirely open ground but for a small isolated tuft of grass in the centre. The puff-adder entered the tuft and proceeded to wind itself round and round in the middle, until it had virtually vanished. I took my eyes away for a moment, and when I looked again, it was with a somewhat uncomfortable feeling I found I could not see the snake at all. Yet the tuft was no more than a few centimetres across.

Cryptic colouration reaches a high degree of development among ground birds, and is one of the two ways in which birds use colouration. Few people would spot the nightjar sitting on her eggs, completely in the open and fully confident of her camouflage. But here it must be taken a step further, for it would be of little advantage if both eggs and chicks were not camouflaged also. Just to cover every eventuality, the Gaboon nightjar can, when sitting, reveal a zig-zag wing pattern that makes it look just like a puff-adder!

[Far left] The striking crest of the Kavirondo crane.

[Left] The cock weaver bird is a handsome golden-yellow and black whilst the hen looks more like a house sparrow.

The second way birds use colour is in courtship or 'epigamic' display. Birds are renowned for their wonderful displays, associated with some of the most beautiful colours in the animal kingdom, sometimes associated with striking adaptations of feathers, as in the Kavirondo, or crowned, crane's headcrest, borne by both cock and hen. However, colour is usually reserved for the cock, such as the cock red-chested sunbird, a crimson and emerald jewel compared to his drab brown hen, who builds an untidy raggle-taggle nest of anything she can find – even scraps of toilet tissue. Among the very common weaverbirds the cock is a handsome golden-yellow and black, whilst the hen looks more like a house sparrow, with only a dusting of yellow on her breast.

Mammals are not so distinguished in this respect, but one example is the lion's black mane. Old naturalist-hunters suggested this was concealing, as when the lion lay in the open the black mane looked like a lump of lava rock. There is little doubt it is a sexual adornment, but it also protects the neck from flailing claws and slashing teeth when two lions fight. Maneless lions lack this protection, but perhaps make up for the lack in other ways, such as the possession of thicker neck skin, or fighting more circumspectly.

There is only one large antelope that shows a marked difference between the male and the female. This is the handsome bull sable antelope, with his jet black, cherry-blossom-boot-polish coat and snow-white dickey. The cow is attractive, too, but in quite a different manner, with her beautiful roan dress. The reason for the difference in colour may be because both buck and doe have prominent horns, which means that the buck can only tell the difference by the colour.

When it comes to wildebeest and hartebeest, both bull and cow have similar horns in both sexes; so how do the cows of these species avoid being attacked by the bulls? Although the adult bulls are darker the cows probably rely on behaviour to avoid aggression; it is a matter of how they hold themselves.

Most antelopes have their patterns, if they have any at all, on their rump, such as the impala with its bold black-and-white design standing out in sharp contrast to its russet body. Some

[Clockwise from above] The lion's mane protects it when fighting.

A sable antelope bull.

A sable antelope bull with its roan cows and young.

Impala does.

A wildebeest with its sandy-coloured calf.

Waterbuck calves are fluffy.

people consider that these patterns enable the animals to follow one another when fleeing danger, but they are more probably connected with social behaviour related to mating.

Earlier some baby animals were described as camouflaged because 'freezing' was their only means of escaping danger. But other babies have quite different colours from those of their parents, yet escape by running with the herd almost immediately after birth. An example is the wildebeest calf whose mother gives birth in open view, often fighting off hyaenas and jackals as she does so. The sandy-coloured, black-faced baby is quite different in appearance from the slate-grey adult. Its colour is hardly likely to be connected with camouflage, so it may be to elicit protective responses, inhibiting attack by bulls. Animal psychologists have found that animals, and particularly humans, respond to baby features such as the snub nose of a human or rabbit baby, or fluffiness, such as the coat of a young waterbuck calf. Most of us think the youngling looks 'sweet', and want to cuddle it. This response is particularly strong in humans because of the long period of attachment to the child. It is possible that the same psychological motivations could be involved in colour patterns such as that of the young wildebeest.

In the sable antelope the young bulls are the same colour as the cows. Perhaps this explains the colour difference in this species, for, looking like the cows, the young bulls do not elicit antagonism from the adult bulls. But every case requires separate consideration. The charming

A zebra mare with her newborn foal.

baby Burchell's zebra has fluffy brown stripes, not black like those of its parents (although the newborn's stripes may look black at birth, when the foal is still wet), but the brown colouring may simply be due to the chemical reaction that produces the black colour not being completed until shortly after birth.

From time to time oddities like black leopards, white impalas, and even white giraffes and a white dik-dik, are reported; in the 1920s there was a herd of 60–70 white waterbuck in northern Kenya. But these are just freaks, although there is a tendency for large mammals to be light in colour in hot, dry areas, and dark in cold, wet areas. So we find blond-maned lions in northern Uganda, and black leopards in Kenya's mountain forests.

Birds provide us with some colour oddities. The countless numbers of lesser and greater flamingo encircling the shores of Kenya's Rift Valley soda lakes like a giant pink candy cake frill owe their beautiful colour to a pigment called carotenoid. This pigment, which is what

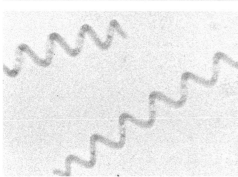

[From top]

Flamingos, 'like a giant pink candy cake frill'.

Carmine bee eaters at a nesting site.

Arthrospira platensis under the microscope. The food of flamingos.

gives carrots their colour, can only be manufactured by plants, and animals must extract it from them. The flamingo's pink depends upon how much it can extract, just as if we were to eat nothing but raw carrots our skin would turn yellow (not pink, though) from the uptake of pigment. The flamingo's source of supply is minute traces of the organic pigment carotenoid present in a microscopic blue-green alga spirulina, *Arthrospira platensis*. Under the microscope this alga looks like a little corkscrew. Its numbers depend upon the alkalinity of the water, which in turn depends upon the rainfall. Likewise the colours of the flamingo are seen to fluctuate from white to rosy pink. The exception is the crimson feathers under the wing, which always retain their deep colour. Evident only when the bird opens its wings, especially in flight, these are used in courtship display; the cock bird stands before the hen and rapidly opens and closes his wings, displaying this bright colour. Spirulina is now regarded as a super-food with many healthful benefits for humans; not least among its dietary benefits it contains over 3,000 per cent more beta-carotene than do carrots.

Another colourful species that lives in groups is the carmine bee-eater, the little birds looking like iridescent jewels with their shining scarlet and green plumage. As they nest in holes in the ground of river banks or cliffs which they dig out, sometimes up to 2.4 metres long, their colours must be for social purposes, not for camouflage.

Even more remarkable when it comes to bird colour are the turacos. These handsome crested birds have two pigments peculiar to them and to no other living creature, as far as we know. One is a brilliant green called turacoverdin, seen in Livingstone's turaco. The other is a bright crimson, turacin, seen in Ross's turaco, which is soluble in alkaline water. Its water-solubility was discovered by a Frenchman in South Africa in 1818; he caught a rain-sodden specimen in a thunderstorm and found to his astonishment that it coloured his hands 'red like blood'. Since then it has always been said the turaco's red colour washes out when it rains, but this is not strictly true, although it could happen if the rain was alkaline enough. Turacoverdin is less soluble.

Remarkable as birds are, it is among the insects, and particularly the butterflies, that the most striking examples of colouration are found. In the previous chapter the separation, or growing apart, of animal species was discussed. Here we find quite the opposite, with many species growing to resemble, or mimic, one another.

[Far left] Livingstone's turaco.

[Left] A camouflaged moth.

Colourful butterflies of the African forest.

Africa is relatively poor in butterfly species, with only some 3,650. The major share goes to South America, with some 7,700, and Asia, with some 4,800. Yet Africa has more cases of mimicry than any of the other regions. Mimicry in this sense is of two kinds: Batesian, named after Bates, the 19th-century naturalist-explorer who accompanied Alfred Russel Wallace to the Amazon and was the first to point out, from observing butterflies there, that a distasteful butterfly was copied in its looks by others which are good to eat; and Müllerian, called after another 19th-century naturalist who went to live in South America, and explained the reason why several distasteful species all have the same colouration: the advantage of this is that by sharing a common and easily learned signal, the losses of some individuals to the inexperienced predators that have not yet learned of the unpleasantness the pattern predicts, are spread among several species. In addition, having fewer patterns to learn, the predators learn more quickly.

The most extraordinary case of butterfly mimicry is shown by a large yellow swallowtail, the mocker-swallowtail, *Papilio dardanus*. The male always looks the same, but the female may have any one of 15 different forms, all mimicking distasteful species. Now if the distasteful model is a rare species, there is not much advantage to be gained by copying it too frequently, as birds and other predators would soon find out they were being duped. So the mocker-swallowtail in Nairobi has seven different female forms, as no particular pattern is selected for. This is because the model, a black and white butterfly called the 'layman', *Amauris albimaculata*, is rare. But in Uganda's Entebbe the mocker-swallowtail has only two forms as there are eight different distasteful models. In Madagascar there is only one female form, and that is exactly the same as the male.

Complicated? Well, let us look at the monarch butterfly, *Danaus*, which has been called the commonest butterfly in the world (although it rarely occurs in Britain). The monarch is slow-flying, conspicuous, and distasteful. Consequently it is an ideal model to mimic, and at least 19 mimics have been recorded. One is the white-barred Acraea, *Acraea encedon*, a common African butterfly which rests at night in the grass in colonies. A further peculiarity is that some of these colonies consist almost entirely of females, whilst others have more equal sex ratios. The monarch itself is the common orange-brown butterfly with black-tipped wings with a white bar across them, which you see everywhere in Africa … or is it one of the mimics you are looking at?

Butterflies do not just mimic one another. There are even those which have forms in the wet season that are different in colour, and sometimes in size, from those in the dry season. Collectors once thought they were different species. Such a butterfly, the gaudy commodore, *Precis octavia*, is a close relative of the English red admiral. It is purple in the dry season, and salmon pink in the wet. But it is the dry season physiology which produces the wet season form, and the wet the dry, for those eggs laid in the dry season result in the wet season form, and those laid in the wet season result in the dry season form.

When it comes to plain, straightforward camouflage, the butterflies and moths are unsurpassed, but they have had 400 million years in which to perfect their colourings. The large East African hawk moth, *Xanthepan morgani*, with a wingspan of over 15 cm, is almost completely invisible as it rests on the bark of a tree. It even aligns the dark streaks on its wings with the dark streaks of the bark. Try gently turning one at right angles (if you can spot one!), and it will immediately turn itself back in line again. There are many excellent examples of this type of concealment to be found in almost any country.

For sheer beauty of colour my favourites are the charaxes: large, fat-bodied, swift-flying forest butterflies allied to the rare purple emperor of English woodlands. Although their upper wings are brilliantly coloured, when they settle their camouflaged underwings make them almost indistinguishable from their background. Unfortunately for the charaxes they have a great weakness for evil-smelling leopard and other carnivore dung. I once found a beautiful specimen in a glade of the Budongo Forest, Uganda. So intoxicated was it with its meal of dung I had to beat it with a pencil to make it open its wings for a photograph. Anyone who has tried to catch these incredibly swift fliers on the wing will appreciate just hew intoxicated this specimen must have been! When I was in Bangui, capital of the Central African Republic, people did a good trade in colourful forest butterflies, creating pictures from their wings. The butterflies had been caught in forest openings by falling for rotting banana pulp spiced with insecticide.

5

Animal weapons

What mammals may lack in colour they certainly make up for in armament. The beauty and diversity of horns and tusks which endow some mammals have long evoked admiration as symbols of masculine beauty, giving rise to the great era of big game hunting in Africa, an activity which today is almost as popular as ever. Despite the fact that most people now find the idea of such pointless collection of 'trophies' distasteful, the storerooms of taxidermists are stacked to the ceilings in America and France in particular, where its adherents are undiminished in number.

Before they evolved horns, animals relied upon their teeth, tusks for stabbing and seizing prey having evolved 90 million years ago. Animals like the lion still use only their teeth and claws as weapons of offence, but as these must also serve the very utilitarian purpose of catching food they show no exaggerated development for threat purposes. This is unlike the dog baboon, whose prominent canines are almost solely for threat and fighting. They are even grooved like a dagger, so they can be quickly withdrawn after stabbing an opponent, the groove releasing the suction. The lion's canine teeth, on the other hand, being smooth, are less easy to pull out once sunk into their prey.

A great concourse of animals relying on its teeth is the rodents: rats, mice, and their allies. Anyone who has picked up an angry mouse knows how effective the chisel-like incisor teeth are. Most rodents found no necessity to develop further protection, with a notable exception being the porcupine. Big as rodents go, the porcupine would make a succulent dish for carnivores if not protected by its battery of sharp quills, which are nothing more than modified hairs. If attacked the porcupine does not run away; it runs backwards into its attacker, leaving a mass of the easily-detachable quills sticking in the victim like pins in a pincushion. With such effective protection it is not surprising to find its skin is very delicate.

Armed in somewhat similar fashion is another prickly fellow, common in Africa: the hedgehog, an insectivore, and thus far removed from the porcupine. The African hedgehog behaves no differently from its English counterpart; when danger threatens it simply rolls itself

[Left] Baboon. The dog baboon's canine teeth are for fighting, not seizing prey.

[Lower left] The lion's teeth are not easily withdrawn from their prey.

[Left] The porcupine's quills are detachable.

[Lower left] African hedgehogs. Their spines are not detachable.

into a ball and hopes that it will be left alone. Unlike the porcupine's quills, the hedgehog's prickles are not detachable.

By far the most common weapons of offence and defence evolved are modifications of the teeth and the growth of horns. Tusks are nothing more than exaggerated teeth. They may be developed from the incisors, as in the elephant, or from the canines, as in the hippo and warthog.

Horns are of three kinds. There is the rhino's horn, a central structure composed through-out of solid horn. Then there is the more familiar horn of the bovids: the cattle, sheep, goats, and antelopes. Their horns consist of paired outgrowths from the forehead, covered with a permanent horny sheath, from the simple pointed horns of a cow to the elaborate horns of the greater kudu. These animals are sometimes known as 'hollowhorned ruminants', although their horns are not really hollow for as well as bone they have tissues and blood inside.

[Above] A trio of hippos displays his ferocious canines.

[Left] Bull elephants carry conspicuous tusks.

Finally there is the giraffe's 'horn'. Not really a horn at all but serving the same purpose, are its paired bony outgrowths on the skull. The bones are covered in skin and not horn, but the name is popularly retained through long usage even though the scientific name for them is ossicones, 'bone cones'.

Another type of armament, not found in Africa, is the deer antler. Like the giraffe's horn it is a bone structure covered with skin, but the deer's 'velvet' is rubbed off when the antler has grown each year, and then months later, after the rut, the entire antler is shed and a new one grown again.

Such variety of weapons has created much speculation concerning how useful they might be. Darwin started the ball rolling with the belief that the animals with the best weapons would be most likely to succeed in combats for winning females, or in survival against predators. These victors would be selected and give rise to offspring with even bigger and better horns, and so on. We now know that inheritance does not work like this, and neither does natural selection.

[Clockwise from top left]

The warthog's tushes are for burrowing.

The giraffe's horns are adapted to its mode of fighting.

The greater kudu's ornate horns.

The rhino's horn is designed to withstand great stress.

A buffalo with record horns.

The finest-looking animals are by no means the boldest. I proved this to myself in the Queen Elizabeth Park, Uganda. There was a buffalo there in 1967 with immense horns, close to the world record of 1.626 metres across (which in fact is held by a cow and not a bull). Remarkable as this buffalo looked, he was of inferior rank to his fellows, always moving aside when they approached him. Contrary to Darwin's view it seems that the most aggressive buffaloes are those with the smallest horns. The more aggressive the animal the more it uses its horns, and so they become broken, worn, and blunted. Exaggerated size is of little use for the buffalo.

The finest male waterbuck I ever saw was also so timid that I was never able to get close enough to photograph it.

Size is not necessarily of value in the animal kingdom. Horn size apart, the larger the species the more timid it usually is. The giant forest hog is twice the size of the warthog, and

[Right] The giant or Lord Derby's eland.

[Lower right] An eland bull.

twice as timid. Largest of all the antelopes, the eland is the first to run at the slightest hint of danger. You can be almost a kilometre distant when, all jowl and jelly-wobble, it takes off across the plains, rolls of muscle jiggling all over like a portly lady running for a bus. Its larger forest-dwelling cousin, the giant or Lord Derby's eland, is just as timid, skulking in cover and full of suspicion of its surroundings.

But Charles Darwin, the great Victorian naturalist who, stimulated as a boy by reading *The Wonders of the World in Nature, Art, and Mind*, told us how evolution worked – that is, how one plant or animal form could produce other different, and more efficient, forms – was careful to point out that each animal would use its horns in its own particular manner. Thus we should consider each as an individual before we start asking ourselves such questions as: Why should a hartebeest's horns be different to those of a wildebeest? Or those of a topi? We will learn little of their purpose looking at pictures of a multitude of forms ranged side by side. Nor from rows and rows of dusty heads in museum galleries. We cannot assign any one cause or function to all animal weapons. To try and establish its function we must consider the whole animal, not just its head.

It has been suggested there must be an optimum shape and size for ungulate horns. So the wide variety – no two species having the same – is inexplicable in the face of the fact that horns seem to be important structures. They have persisted since Eocene times and have evolved separately in different groups of animals. But one could equally argue there must be an optimum shape and size for an ungulate. However, ungulates show just as great a diversity of body shape and size as they do of their horns.

Herein lies the answer, for we can guess these ungulates have each evolved to fill different niches in the environment. Likewise their horns have evolved to fit each individual's particular requirements. Hartebeest have evolved into several forms, each with their own distinctive horns, which must imply that they also have developed variations in fighting.

[Clockwise from top left]
The kongoni hartebeest.
The topi.
The Lelwel hartebeest.

[Above] 'Gertie' of Amboseli, a docile rhino with a record-length horn, clearly not used for fighting and indicating the animal's mild temperament.

[Left] Rhinos can break off their horn by warding off the unwanted attentions of bulls, but this one still has a large second horn.

The rhino's horn is not a primitive hangover, but an interesting example of adaptation to withstand extreme stresses. The rhino's method of attack is to charge its adversary, using the horn as a battering ram. The average black rhino weighs one and a half tonnes and can charge at 40 kph. Mathematics tell us that if it is brought to a halt within 0.3 metres after striking an object, the effective impact per square centimetre on the end of its horn is something like 9.3 tonnes! This force is rapidly dissipated down the length of the horn but nonetheless represents an enormous pressure on an organic structure.

We can now see why the rhino's horn is as it is. A hollow bovid-type horn could not withstand such a shock and would splinter on impact. As it grows from the base, the bovid horn's exterior dying as soon as it has hardened, the horn could never grow to a point again. When breakage does occasionally happen, as in waterbuck for example, maggots infect the end of the exposed bone. But if the rhino snaps the end off his horn he can easily sharpen it up again; the tissue is quite dead and insensitive. This would not be so if it was made of bone, which is a living tissue with a blood supply. An antler is composed of dead bone in its final stages, but it is much more brittle than horn. This is why antlers are regrown each year, for they would not last a lifetime.

The rhino too has a safety valve; if the impact is too great the entire horn can be torn off. Perhaps a painful procedure, but one that does the rhino no permanent harm, as it can grow another from the base. Possessed of a second, posterior horn (some individuals even have a third small bump), it is not left defenceless, although sometimes rhinos lose both horns. The Indian rhino has only one, quite small, horn, but it does not use it for fighting. Perhaps the Indian rhino's greater size – an adult bull can weigh well over 2 tonnes – surpasses the capabilities of horn, in that the impact of a charge would be too great for it. Instead its main weapons are its sharp lower canine teeth, which in the African rhino are either rudimentary or absent altogether.

The rhino horn has one other specialization. All animal horns, hooves, nails and claws are composed of a tubular substance called keratin, chemically similar to hair. The rhino's horn is often wrongly described as a 'mass of hair cemented together' or 'matted hair', as it sometimes becomes very frayed at the base. Microscopic examination has shown that this is because it lacks the 'cement' other horns have to bind the tubules together. This probably gives the rhino horn an added elasticity, making it less likely to shatter on impact.

Unlike the rhino's battering ram, the enormous impenetrable boss shielding the buffalo's forehead is not an offensive weapon. It is to protect the buffalo's own braincase. If it did not have this armour-plating, the tremendous impact that its head receives from the beast's tonne of muscle striking an opponent would smash its own skull as if it was an eggshell. But in fact, when two buffaloes fight they do not charge each other head to head; instead, once they've got in close, they use their horns as hooks. The most important part of the buffalo's offensive armament is the upcurving tip of its horn, with which it tries to rip and gouge. A game warden described to me how he once witnessed an old buffalo spin its opponent clean onto its back with a quick hook. I have seen one with the horn on one side completely torn off, presumably from an over-zealous hook. In Uganda there were two cases in one year of buffaloes that had got their horns inextricably locked together in fighting. In one case the unfortunate animals were shot, and in the other an enterprising scientist sawed the end off one horn. This released the combatants, who ungratefully switched their attack to the scientist's vehicle.

Buffalo show such a tremendous variety in shape and size, hardly two animals in the same herd having the same curvature to their horns. This is partly due to the stage of growth, but the cows, not being prone to fighting in the same manner as the bulls, lack the reinforced boss across the forehead, which is more important in fighting than is the shape of the horns.

Antelope horns, with their multitude of forms but all following the basic pattern of an expanding spiral, present a more confusing picture. To make anything of it, several factors concerning each animal must be considered.

Firstly, does the animal live in the forest, in the bush, or in the open? A habitual dweller in forest and thick scrub, like the bushbuck, has only short, sharp horns that do not hinder

A dik-dik. It has short spikes for horns, all that it needs.

its passage in the undergrowth. The short spikes of the dik-dik buck are used in fighting one another, and those horns, having no twists or turns, do not get tangled in undergrowth either.

Another consideration is how gregarious is an animal. Those living in large herds, like wildebeest and topi, have relatively compact horns, not likely to stick into other herd members when they jostle together. In those animals with very elaborate horns, such as the greater kudu, the does are hornless.

Then we must consider the enemies an animal needs to contend with. A Thomson's gazelle is hardly likely to have horns that will protect it from a lion or leopard, against which predators it is helpless once caught. Those of the oryx do seem for defence against such predators; both sexes have horns and use them dexterously when attacked, twisting the head if an attacker charges, to try and impale it on their points. Oryx and kudu, meanwhile, have only to hold their heads back and their horns lie on either side of the nape of the neck, hindering a lion or leopard from seizing it.

When for defence, horns are usually present in both sexes; but, as we saw, some does have them even if they do serve primarily a social function. Whereas this may be related to the protection of young bulls, an adult bull thus unable to tell the difference between a young bull and an adult doe, it could also be that in such cases they represent a neutral character in the doe and no selection pressure operates against them. When does bear functionless horns, in the sense of weapons, they are always much less developed than those of the bucks. In the Thomson's gazelle doe they are so fragile they sometimes break off if the animal falls over! Occasionally hornless females develop freak spindly horns due to hormone imbalance. This may be seen in kob and waterbuck.

Both giraffe sexes are horned, although only the bull uses them, and in the cow they are much reduced. Often described as 'primitive', the horns are on the contrary specialized structures, admirably adapted to the bull's method of fighting with his fellows; he uses his head as a club, trying to strike his opponent with the horns by swinging his neck over and backwards in an arc. The cow's horns and skull are, however, far too delicate for this; if she has to defend herself she does so by kicking very effectively with her forefeet, and a kick can kill a lion.

[From top]

The cow greater kudu is hornless.

Impala does are hornless.

A gemsbok bull. It is the southern African version of the oryx.

The greater kudu bull with its magnificent horns.

Horns in a male alone suggest that their function is social, used for fighting other males of the same species, or perhaps merely to impress the opposite sex. It is in the latter that the most exaggerated developments are found, such as the magnificent spiral horns of the greater kudu, and the cow is in no doubt as to what sex her partner is. But in the oryx, where both sexes are horned, courting preliminaries consist of a trial of strength to determine who they are dealing with. If two bulls come together this results in a fight, but when the sexes are opposite the bull finds himself much stronger than the cow. Thus not only how an animal fights, but how it courts, may influence horn shape.

The oryx fights on its knees, trying to stick the points of its horns under its opponent to expose the belly. The waterbuck lunges like a fencer and the sable antelope hooks upwards, so the waterbuck's horns curve forwards and the sable's backwards. Horns are never merely decorative for decoration's sake; the twists and spirals all result from natural laws of growth.

The function of ridges or annuli is not clear to me. They may be strengthening devices, or non-slip devices, preventing the horns simply sliding over one another when two animals clash. In temperate regions the ridges can be related to seasonal growth, but in tropical animals they are simply related to horn length, showing no obvious seasonal fluctuations.

Another animal weapon able to withstand stress is the elephant's tusk. It is of the same basic composition as other teeth, but with the microscopic dentinal tubules, of which teeth and ivory are composed, arranged in wavy bands. Apparent only when the structure grows long enough, these bands give true ivory its characteristic 'engineturned' appearance, imparting to it a kind of two-way stretch, making ivory one of the most perfectly elastic substances known, which is why it was so sought after for billiard balls in the 19th century. A leading London supplier boasted that an average of five balls were cut from each tusk and the average sale was 950 balls per month – equivalent to 95 elephants, or 1,140 a year.

[Right] Both bull and cow gemsbok and oryx have similar horns.

[Below] A billiard ball mountain representing the death of 1,140 elephants per year. (Photo: Burroughes & Watts. n.d., (1889). *Billiards Simplified*. London: Burroughes & Watts.)

Even so, despite their elasticity tusks are often broken, for they are subjected to tremendous stresses, such as when a bull elephant exerts his 4 tonnes on them to lever over a tree. Elephants tend to be 'right-handed' and it is often the right tusk that is broken. In fighting, an elephant uses its tusks for jabbing an opponent at close quarters, and a considerable force is exerted on the tusk should it meet with resistance. Bull elephants not infrequently kill one another; one dead bull was found with its opponent's tusk in its chest, broken into four pieces from the impact of the thrust!

Warthog tusks have very much a twofold function, used in fighting and of great importance for burrowing. (Contrary, however, to what was once thought, they are of little importance for rooting out food; for that, like all pigs, it uses its snout.) As it is a hairless animal, the temperature of even an African night can fall too low for the warthog, so if it cannot snuggle into an underground burrow it has a good chance of dying from pneumonia. The upper, stouter tusks are the main burrowing tools, the sharp-pointed lower ones being used for defence or fighting.

When warthogs fight they push forehead to forehead with all of their might, and each tries to pull its head away and deliver a sideways swing at its opponent. If successful it creates a resounding thud against the opponent's tough skull, which can be heard for quite a distance. The sharp lower tusks inflict nasty wounds in this sideways swing, and the function of the warts – so characteristic of the warthog's ugly face – to protect the eyes, becomes obvious. Although fighting is confined to the boars, you cannot tell the difference between the sexes in younger animals from the size of their tusks – a clear indication of their important function for burrowing.

When all the factors that can influence the shape and size of an animal's weapons are taken into consideration, the variety is hardly surprising. It is also clear that one animal's pattern is not necessarily suitable for another. But the development of these weapons does not imply nature 'red in tooth and claw', as the Victorian naturalists liked to describe it – a constant bloody battle between species. But neither is it the league of friendship many modern biologists would like us to

[Top] Waterbuck fight to kill.

[Above] Kob fighting. A lesser buck, extreme left, pairs with a doe while the dominant bucks are distracted fighting.

Bull elephants have prominent tusks.

believe. Some animals probably use their weapons only for bluff, but equally there are those that use them with the sole intent of killing any opponent that does not give way. I have often found cases of death from fighting among waterbuck, Uganda kob, and hippo. The latter are frequently seen with appalling wounds. Even the docile-looking impala rams often kill one another. Such deaths may be rarely witnessed, but that does not mean they are not taking place. In nearly three years' field study of waterbuck in Uganda I was witness to only two violent fights between bucks, neither of which had serious outcomes. But the scarred necks and torn ears of virtually every adult buck testified that fights were much more common than my observations suggested.

Weapons would not have developed as they have if they were not used to good advantage. Nevertheless owners always like to try bluff first. Notable among the bluffers is the elephant, which will resort to all manner of display – swishing its trunk around, erecting its ears, and trumpeting defiantly – before actually charging. I once witnessed an extraordinary display by a young bull which, having gone through all the usual head-shaking, suddenly knelt on all fours

[Right] A bull hippo displays his canines in threat.

[Lower right] The hippo has the widest gape of any land mammal.

Another hippo displays his canines.

and, lifting one foreleg, pawed the air with it, at the same time holding its mouth open with its trunk curled back over its head, just as if it had been a trained circus elephant.

The hippo bull is always opening his mouth in cavernous yawns. This is not because he is tired, but to show off his ferocious canines. Constantly rearing out of the water, the bulls open their mouths as wide as they can in a warning to others. They must have the widest gape of any living mammal, a gape that they have no use for other than for display, as, feeding on grass, they crop it keeping their jaws fairly close together. Vicious fighting takes place when neither party is intimidated by such displays. Approach a hippo too closely on land and he will warn you, opening his mouth and waving his head from side to side. It certainly serves the purpose of keeping an intruder at a distance, even if the hippo is only bluffing. But an animal that bluffs is torn between a desire to attack and to flee. That is, it is not so frightened that it will flee, and the balance can easily be tipped in the other direction. So if you ignore his warning the hippo is just as likely to attack as to run away. Be warned. One is even recorded as biting a cyclist in two, bicycle and all!

6

Living together

Our journey onto the plains of Africa showed us that not only were the numbers of large animals striking, but also their great variety of forms, all living together in apparent harmony. This seemingly good neighbourliness is because each species has its own lifestyle. Thus the kob buck has a small territory of not more than 15–35 metres across, where he shows off to attract the does and repel all other male intruders; but away from his own patch (and that of any other buck) he mixes in harmony. The waterbuck has a much larger territory, which supplies his yearround living requirements and to which the does are attracted for food and water. Unlike the kob, in which the strongest bucks are those with territories in the centre of the arena, the strongest waterbucks may be those whose territory includes water. The waterbuck drinks daily, and to do so weaker bucks, who come from inland where there is less competition for areas, must make a daily journey through the territories of the stronger. When passing through the waterside owners' territories they must show suitable respect, otherwise they will be attacked and unable to drink. So they pass through with heads held low.

Whereas the territory of the kob is for showing off, the waterbuck's is his home and his castle. The does wander through at will and do not visit the bucks for mating. Kob does, in contrast, live in the area which harbours the bucks' territories. A buck does not display every time he sees a herd of does, but will approach them to see if any are willing to pair. The hartebeest operates a similar system, whilst the wildebeest has a system falling between that of the kob and the waterbuck.

In the Ngorongoro Crater of Tanzania, where the wildebeest population is resident throughout the year, each bull carves himself out an area of about 100 metres diameter. Somewhere in this he has a favourite spot or stamping-ground, worn bare from digging and rubbing his face gland on the ground, and covered with his droppings. On the adjacent Serengeti plains the vast herds of wildebeest are nomadic, constantly on the move. But they must halt sometimes, for watering, feeding, ruminating, or resting. When they do, all is frantic activity. The bulls, which have been tagging along in quiet acquiescence, suddenly become

[Above] Impala does.

[Right] A duiker buck.

animated. Cavorting hither and thither they rapidly organize a territory around themselves within which each of them herds a group of cows, a behaviour that earned the wildebeest the name of 'clown of the plains', as early observers did not realize what was going on. When, as if by some common signal, the herd moves on again, the bulls abandon their jealous behaviour and tag along together again quite amicably.

But whereas the kobs rigidly respect their territorial boundaries, when cow wildebeest are ready to pair it becomes a free-for-all. The territory owner frantically tries to keep invading bulls at bay, and at the same time win the attentions of the cow. But whereas both kob and

Uganda waterbuck have either a long breeding season or breed throughout the year, most of the wildebeest breeding is confined to one short period: the rut. Despite the scrimmage, all the strong bulls are likely to have a chance of mating.

There are many variations of social organization. Impala rams defend a herd rather than an area, whilst the black rhinoceros bull has a home range rather than a territory, sharing parts of it with other bulls. At the other extreme the pugnacious little buck bush duiker defends his territory against all comers. He meets his opposite sex for one purpose: to mate. That accomplished, the erstwhile lovers will, if kept together, fight like fury.

Lions were once fondly believed to pair for life, but nothing could be further from the truth. They live in prides, family units of both males and females, the males defending the shared territory against other prides. A male will mate with any female in the pride but does not stay with her. The sub-dominant males, when adult, leave to try to take over another pride's territory, and if successful in driving out the dominant male are accepted by the females.

As trespassing can result in serious consequences, how does one animal know where another's territory begins and ends? Well, it is up to the owner to advertise themself. They do this by using sound, sight, scent, or combinations of these.

Sight is used by brightly coloured fishes, such as those of coral reefs. In our terrestrial habitat sight is used by a range of animals from lizards to birds and monkeys; the male agama lizard, for example, sits on top of an anthill nodding his bright blue head for all to see, but the female is camouflaged like lichen. It has been suggested that the colours of some antelopes may be connected with this advertising purpose; the male topi, for example, by standing on top of a termite mound, may be advertising his presence in his territory, his dark colouring making him stand out against the skyline.

A male agama lizard advertising himself on a termite mound. The bright blue may attract insects as well as being a warning to other males.

[From top]

The female agama lizard is camouflaged like lichen.

A fish eagle calling from its nest.

A pair of handsome fish eagles survey their territory.

But if you cannot make yourself seen very easily, then you can make yourself heard. The most vociferous exponent of this type of territorial advertising is the fish eagle, most beautiful of the raptors and also the noisiest. Its penetrating cry is one of the unforgettable sounds of Africa, heard ringing out over the water from dawn to dusk, and even during the dead of night. The paired birds constantly call back and forth, whether the hen is sitting and her mate hunting, or whether both are wheeling in the sky. Extraordinary effort is put into making the cry even in flight, the head being thrown right back onto the body. Thus between themselves fish eagles can practise a sort of audible radar; if the signals between other pairs become too loud they know they are getting into foreign waters and retreat accordingly. The centre of their territory is probably the large, untidy nest, usually surmounting a candelabrum euphorbia tree. From this vantage point the handsome black-and-white bird with its chestnut stole flies out over the water to snatch at a surfacing fish. Basking tilapia are the usual victims. I have seen a fish eagle seize a fish so large that it could not lift it, and rather than release its prize, the eagle rowed itself ashore with its wings. There is a story that the same pair occupied the same nest site at Entebbe on the shores of Lake Victoria for over 19 years. But like the robin in an English garden, without the birds being marked distinctively in some way, one cannot know whether or not it was a succession of different birds looking the same.

Wherever you hear the cry of the fish eagle you are also likely to hear the call of another territorial animal, the hippo. During the day you might want to laugh when hippo after hippo raises its head in some muddy wallow and croaks its defiance, often ending in a choking splutter. But if you are sitting out on a moonlit night, the sight of the oily-black bodies laboriously hauling themselves onto land to wend into the darkness combine with the sound of their booming grunts echoing across the water to make one of the unforgettable memories of Africa.

Away from the water, just as the fish eagle is the most vociferous bird of prey, so is the sedentary bull wildebeest the most vociferous of antelopes, continually advertising his territory with loud grunting. The Uganda kob advertises by whistling, squeezing in its whole abdomen as it forces air out through its mouth in a most unantelopelike sound. By this means others are made aware that a territorial owner is near and that they will be met with resistance if they approach any closer.

Another well-known vocal member of the plains is the lion. It is an old belief that the lion roars at night to stampede its prey, whereas in fact the roar is used to communicate between lions and to advertise territory. I had a convincing demonstration of this in the Queen Elizabeth Park, when a companion wanted to record lions roaring. One night a pride of 16 lionesses was reported lying by the side of a road, so out we went with our recording equipment. We planned to play a hyaena recording to them in the hope this would induce them to roar. The pride was found, stretched out in languorous repose, and we played the recording. In the spotlight we could see one lioness blink an eye, but that was all. We were about to try again, when at that moment, far, far away, in the distance I heard the – barely audible to me – sound of a lion's roar. Instantly pandemonium broke loose as the whole pride, within but a few feet of us, answered in disjointed chorus. It has been said the lion stands to roar, and points its mouth at the ground. But these did not even move their positions, some lying on their sides roaring away with eyes closed as if dreaming in their sleep.

Taken by surprise, my companion fumbled furiously with the recorder, but by the time it was running they had subsided into silence. Then in the distance, the barely audible answer was heard. Once again bedlam broke forth from the pride. And so, back and forth, went the lions' vocal tom-tom, until it was quite clear to them who was where. But as you may imagine, 16 lusty lionesses bellowing in unison into a microphone from some 3 metres away did not produce a very good recording!

The most common method of territorial advertisement among mammals is scent marking, often used in conjunction with vocal methods. We find that in this respect the lion has rather dirty habits, for he appears to mark his presence with urine, either spraying a bush and then rubbing his face in it, or urinating on the ground and rubbing his hind feet in it. In fact he is spraying scent from his anal glands, although it may often be followed by urinating, and sometimes he will urinate while scraping with the hind feet, thus distributing the urine scent along the trail. Then if another lion comes upon such an 'I was here' signal, he covers it with his own.

Anyone captivated by the charming presence of the bushbaby has invariably been somewhat disillusioned when they have released their pet into a nice clean room. The bushbaby promptly urinates onto its hands, and then rubs them over all and sundry until everything has the nice homely odour of bushbaby urine.

The black rhino uses droppings to mark out its home range. Experiments carried out by a scientist in the Ngorongoro Crater showed that a rhino will follow a cloth bag of faeces dragged behind a car, like a hound on a drag hunt. But as the rhino's area is a home range, rather than a territory, the dung piles that mark out the area are communal, and several rhinos will contribute to each pile. The rhino's habit of breaking up its droppings is well known, and another animal which does likewise is the hippo, with a flattened spatula-like tail seemingly specially made for the purpose. But whereas the rhino passes its dung and then scatters it with a kicking motion of its hind legs like a dog, the hippo whisks its flattened tail from side to side when defecating, producing a shower of dung over all and sundry. On land it chooses bushes for its signpost, repeatedly using the same ones, and dung heaps can reach a large size, being contributed to by any passing hippo, thus they are not individual territorial markers. Hippos are said to be territorial only in water, where a bull defends a territory consisting of a strip of shoreline and a narrow strip of bank against other bulls if they challenge the holder, otherwise the latter tolerates them. Those bulls that are not territory holders form bachelor groups, often within a territory, and then there are the cow groups, the sexes generally remaining separate. Although not believed to be territorial on land, carcasses of hippos that have clearly died fighting suggest territorial disputes on land as well as in water.

Urine and faecal markers do not rely on their own smell but are anointed by various glands as they are passed out by the animal. One of the most well known of these is the civet cat's anal gland. Well known because its contents are the basis of high-class ladies' perfumes, being more politely known as a 'musk gland' in the trade. Small carnivores such as the genet cat become very interested in ladies wearing such scents, despite the many processes the musk has gone through since extraction.

If you come across a pile of whitened husks of dead millipede skins in the African bush, this is a civet cat's signpost. One of the favourite foods of the civet, whose face reminds one of a

[Left] A civet cat.

[Lower left] An oribi buck. The functions of its many glands are unknown.

Disney robber character, is the large African millipede, which reaches over 15 cm in length. Its tough exoskeleton is indigestible, and the large accumulations of it, anointed by the civet cat's anal gland, are easily found.

Although marking with urine and droppings is common, many animals have multiple arrangements of scent glands to serve various purposes. Among ungulates it is the smaller animals that have, as a rule, the more complicated scent glands. Down among the grass stems it is a world of smells for the duiker; as it isn't likely to see others of its kind until it is on top of them, smell is more important than sight. The duiker has three obvious sets of glands: a pair in front of the eyes, marked by a black line, a pair in the inguinal (groin) region, and a pair between the hooves. Watch a buck duiker at home and you will notice an almost imperceptible anointing of stems with its facial gland as it moves about. This slight movement is unlike that of the oribi, an antelope of similar size.

The oribi is a territorial animal of tall grassland. The local people will tell you it is only found in short grass areas, but the simple fact is that it is more easily seen when the grass is short. In long grass it is a stealthy animal, creeping away when disturbed, instead of bounding into the air as it does when fleeing in the open, 'ruffing' its white rump patch, i.e. standing it erect, for all to see. One early writer stated that oribi lived in pairs and when flushed dashed away for some 50 metres before rising on their hind legs, but I never saw this and in addition I mostly encountered them singly. It has a much larger facial gland than the duiker, pouch-like and producing a black, tarry substance. It also has glands between all of its toes, plus inguinal glands and a pair of glandular patches beneath the ears. When the oribi buck marks his territory he first bites the top off a stalk and then pushes his facial gland over the tip, leaving it covered with the black, sticky substance. This is his territorial signpost; but the functions of his other glands are more of a mystery.

Only in an American animal, the black-tailed deer, has any idea of multiple gland function been determined. This animal has facial glands, glands between its toes, and glands on its ankles. Those between its toes seem important for individual recognition, whilst the ankle glands discharge when the animal is alarmed or frightened, a complementary signal to the visual display of exposing the rump pattern. Urine is also important for scent marking in this deer. At this stage we can only guess what the function of equivalent glands in our duiker and oribi might be. As the animal behaviourist Konrad Lorenz put it, mammals mostly 'think through their noses'. Perhaps the most important sense to most of them, scent opens up to them an extraordinary range of experience we can only guess at, let alone imagine.

Searching for chimpanzees in Uganda's Queen Elizabeth National Park Maramagambo Forest, I became aware of a strange, high-pitched twittering noise. As I carefully made my way forward with my African guide, the noise grew louder and louder until the whole air was filled with a deafening cacophony of sound. Looking around for a way down from the rocky cliff on

A cave of fruit bats in Uganda.

which I and my guide found ourselves, I seized some lianas for support and eased my way down the rock face to a streambed, where an astonishing sight met my eyes. There in a cave which lay a little way back from the stream was the cause of all the noise. Inside, thousands upon thousands of bats were crammed together all madly twittering away, from time to time leaving their rocky perches to flutter around inside the cave. Cautiously, I made my way towards the dark, forbidding entrance, and had almost reached it when a brown spotted shape burst out of a recess almost at my feet, nearly bowling me over. It was gone almost before I could let out a yell. It was a young hyaena looking for an easy meal, more frightened than I was.

I tied a handkerchief over my face and entered the mouth of the cave. There was an overpowering sickly stench, and drops of urine rained down upon me as I stood surveying the scene. Everywhere I looked were dense serried rows of hundreds and hundreds of topsy-turvy creatures, now beginning to take fright at my unwonted presence, peeling off in their dozens to whirl round and round my head. The cave was large and mysterious, with pendulous stalactites hanging from the walls and hidden recesses, while in the centre, among a jumble of rocks, a great hole fell away into the darkness. But as I sank to my ankles in the spongy guano I thought twice about exploring further. I was well aware that one can contract a pneumonia-like disease from bat caves, histoplasmosis, caused by the bacterium *Histoplasma capsulatum*, which can be fatal if not treated. It occurs in the guano. The bat was the Egyptian fruit bat, *Rousetta aegyptiacus*.

It left me wondering how the female can find her offspring in a cave among so many thousands of other individuals. Controlled experiments have shown that she does so by smell. Although attracted to any baby bat by its squeaks, she rejects them all until she finds the one with the right odour. This rarely happens in nature as the mother carries the young clinging to her body if she can. But when the bats all return to their cave each day, we must imagine it as either a grand free-for-all to find roosting places, or that each bat knows exactly where to go. Most likely each recognizes its own peg by scent. If true, it means there must be as many variations of the scent as there are bats in the cave!

One might think that the last thing a secretive animal wants to do is leave a tell-tale scent trail behind it with its foot glands, especially if alarmed. Surely this would lead predators right to the animal? Perhaps the scents are not within the range experienced by the predators, or, like the bushbuck's tail alarm signal, a scent can be abruptly switched off, leaving the follower confused at the end of the trail. It seems unlikely there are so many trails criss-crossing one another that the pattern is too bewildering, for we know how well-trained dogs can follow an individual scent.

But imagine a leopard tracking a duiker, and suddenly it comes to a point where the powerful odour of a civet cat has crossed the trail; the leopard would have to make a detour to pick up the duiker's scent again. If this happened two or three times with other such red herrings the leopard would probably soon give up.

The topi bull has a large facial gland with which he marks his territory, getting down on his knees and rubbing it on the ground or on a termite mound, just as the wildebeest does. He also has glands between the toes of the forefeet. But scent glands tend to be reduced in the larger ungulates, which are able to rely more upon their eyes. The extreme example is the giraffe, whose nose is carried well above the world of smells so it has no special scent glands.

Newborn antelope calves appear to be lacking in scent, but among those species which conceal their young after birth, when the mother visits the young regularly to feed it she must surely leave a scent trail leading straight to it. But if the adult scent is likely to be everywhere in the grass, then a predator would have no reason to follow any particular trail.

The waterbuck also lacks a special gland, but both sexes have large smelly grease glands all over the body. As it moves about the waterbuck cannot help leaving a trail behind it, so the territorial buck has no need to actively mark his territory. Let us suppose a waterbuck has ignored the territorial conventions and entered another's domain. He is most likely to be suddenly confronted by the owner galloping towards him. This is the critical moment for the intruder. If he turns tail, then he is run right out of the area. But if he stands his ground, the owner's gallop will slow to a walk, and then to a halt; the owner's bluff number one, the gallop with intent, has failed. It is tempting to think that this has happened because if the owner had not galloped straight on he might not have speared the intruder, but in fact he probably would have. It is in fact because the intruder, by standing still and meeting the owner's challenge, has set in motion another reflex; as the intruder is clearly not easily frightened, the owner must resort to other forms of bluff.

Displaying now takes place, to test the intruder's nerve, consisting of showing off attributes important in fighting. The buck waterbuck neck is extremely muscular, with skin of over 2 cm thick, protecting it from horn wounds. So the owner displays this, holding his neck stiffly and arching it in characteristic manner, like a dressage horse, then inclining his horns towards the opponent. The two may walk around each other, showing off their size and weighing each other up. The opponent may then accept the challenge of the inclined horns, meeting them with his own to test the other's strength. Noses, followed by foreheads, are put together, and a pushing match ensues. The harder they push and resist one another, the more aggressive they become. Each tries to pull away and lunge at the other, like boxers caught in a clinch. Such attempts are immediately countered, and if the opponents are not well matched a bout seldom gets past the pushing stage before one gives up. This is usually the intruder, who is ill at ease on foreign ground. Serious fights follow only between evenly matched individuals, and can result in death if one of the combatants succeeds in horning the other in the body. With over 227 kg of muscle behind the needle-sharp horn points, there is little chance for the receiver if a lunge is not properly parried.

This form of display and fighting, with minor variations, is a fairly basic pattern among antelopes. Some put much more effort into the display, and this is probably related to greater mutual contact so that too much fighting must be avoided. Clearly too much is detrimental to the survival of the species.

When one impala ram challenges another, he erects his white lavatory-brush tail in the air and runs forward in an odd rocking motion, blowing vulgar raspberry-like noises. At the same time the white hairs around the black rump stripe are ruffed.

Ruffing is common among ungulates and is important in social behaviour, occurring in such widelyseparated species as the oribi and the European roe deer. Once together, impala rams test each other's strength and battle much like waterbuck, but their display can lead to an extraordinary sight among the bachelor rams. Watching a herd of 100 or so one evening, I

An impala buck leaping. When it does so its hind leg glands discharge an odour.

saw one erect his tail and, uttering his strange noise, rock after another. The other took to his heels, noisily blowing and displaying also. As they wove in and out among the other rams, so the others joined in. Soon over 100 were rocking back and forth all ever the plain, a galaxy of white lavatory-brush tails waving, and the air filled with their strange noise. Abruptly it petered out almost as quickly as it had begun, and evening feeding was resumed.

Impala are noted for their extraordinary leaping ability, jumping incredible heights and distances when alarmed, sailing with grace and seeming ease, front and hind legs stretched to their limit, the bucks with their lyre-shaped horns laid back. It is believed that when they do this they puff out alarm scent from glands on the hind hocks that are conspicuously marked by a black tuft of hair.

Bachelor herds are an important component of territorial social behaviour. The young bucks must have a place in which to live, and in many species, even if not attacked by the adults, they join together to form their own club. When they come of age they leave it, to try and wrest a territory from an older buck. Usually it is the oldest bucks, past their prime, which are targeted and beaten. But they have probably already been pushed into less favourable areas with advancing years. By starting in one of these a young buck can gradually work his way up to something better as he becomes more skilled in fighting, and more powerful. The oldest bucks are then forced to inhabit even less hospitable areas, where death, in the dry season when times are lean, soon takes its toll.

Territoriality has long been unwittingly observed by hunters and naturalists who have referred to solitary bulls driven from the herd as outcasts. But there is only one common species

I can recall offhand of which this is true, and that is the buffalo. Buffalo are highly gregarious creatures, not happy unless they are jostling one another in close proximity. When they lie down it is side by side; and when they wallow, it is almost on top of one another. In the midst of this scrum is the herd bull, moving about his territory in close contact with his permanent following. Bachelor bulls are also a part of this following, and when one of them becomes strong enough he ousts the herd bull. The erstwhile leader then often becomes a solitary figure, restricted to a small, herdless area. He is not always solitary, though; sometimes old bulls pair up, or even form groups of up to half a dozen or so. But if he does become solitary he also becomes a danger to any passer-by happening upon him accidentally. Solitary buffaloes are renowned for their liability to attack – but is it from fear? Or could it be the desperate defence of the last little piece of ground left to them?

Territorial fighting and display is usually, but not always, the prerogative of the male. So in most species the female adopts a much more docile role in animal societies, for the territorial system often forces her into a more communal life than that of the males. Witness the prides of lions numbering several adult females, all of which show great affection for one another. The schools of fat hippos, lying packed together like sardines; the impala harems; the herds of buffalo cows. There are exceptions to the gregarious life, though; the bushbuck and duiker does, for example, lead just as solitary an existence as the bucks.

The wildebeest bull will stand aside and doze while zebra queue up to roll on his dust patch. He may even share part of his territory with that of a Tommy. If the territory is large, like that of the waterbuck, it may be used by several species. These other species are simply as a part of the environment; no social intercourse takes place between them. Territorial animals are imperialist capitalists. They fight for their estate and then live off the benefits, so territoriality becomes a battle within the species but not among species. With its many variations it is probably the most common social organization among vertebrates. Not only in mammals, it is widespread in birds and fishes, and found also in reptiles, from the crocodile to the wall lizard.

Among birds, however, many exceptions are found, one of the best known being the communal weaverbirds. Trees laden with nests of these weavers are one of the characteristic sights of the African bush. The birds' communal nature even extends to more than one species nesting in the same colony. The cleverly woven nests are the work of the cock, which weaves several in the hope that one will be taken by a hen. It is an amusing sight at nesting time to watch the gaudy black and yellow cock hopping agitatedly from branch to branch. The hen – more sparrow-like in appearance, with a dusting of pale yellow – quite unmoved by his exhortations, carefully examines the little homes one by one, only to fly away altogether if she does not find one to her liking. The nests must be securely woven to the branches if they are to withstand the torrential downpours that occur soon after sitting has begun. The hen's careful inspection before acceptance is a wise precaution, for after the first heavy storm of the season the ground beneath a colony is littered with fallen nests. The more rejections the cock gets, presumably the more nests he builds. So a colony always has a number of empty nests, and these may incidentally offer some protection from hawks, which often swoop on a colony and snatch nests off the branches. Perhaps for this reason the red-chested sunbird, which builds its nest among weaver colonies, often constructs a solid dummy nest just in front of the real one.

[Top] Buffalo are gregarious animals.

[Above] Old bull buffalo are driven from the herd.

Although birds like the weavers show a high degree of togetherness, they are perhaps a dubious exception to the true territorial life, for they can still identify themselves with a unit of property: the nest. But when we consider the fruit bat, the only really communal mammal, all it possesses is a place to hang itself up on. Those in the cave I stumbled upon in Uganda's Maramagambo Forest, crammed so tightly together that every space was occupied, behave quite

Weaver birds nest in colonies.

differently to another species of fruit bat, *Eidolon helvum*, which lives in the heart of Kampala City, Uganda. This bat chooses to roost in the open, in a stand of eucalyptus trees lining a main road. Each evening, as the sun begins to set, they start their nightly exodus. By the time it is dark, half an hour later, the multitudes winging across the sky still seem undiminished. For birds of prey the completely open roosting place would seem like a self-service store, but this does not in fact appear to be so. One sees no predators around the roosting bats, which apparently rely upon the concept of safety in numbers. No predator is likely to be able to eat them all, whether living in the open or in a cave – and an individual can always hope, we might suppose, that it will be its neighbour that is taken and not itself. Perhaps this is the reason these comparatively defenceless creatures band together in such numbers.

Discounting these rather extreme exceptions, living apart is how most animals solve the problem of living together. In Chapter 8 we will look at the reason nearly all animals have to come together at some time or other in their lives: mating and the perpetuation of the species.

7

The killers

There is one group of animals that does not live in harmony with the rest: the carnivores, the killers that prey upon the herbivores (and other carnivores). The large predators are lion, leopard, cheetah, hyaena, and hunting dog. At times these feed on one another, but mainly on ungulates, the antelopes and gazelles, primates, and anything else that offers a meal. A host of smaller predators range in size from jackals such as the black-backed or side-striped and the golden, the size of a fox, downwards. These feed on other small carnivores, on rodents, birds, amphibians, and snakes, but the jackals are also noted for following lions about, to try and scavenge leftovers from their kills. Jackals are very noisy creatures, making high-pitched sounds, but whereas the golden jackal hardly lives up to its name with its scruffy, dour looks, the apparent charm of the black-backed jackal belies its real nature.

[Far left] A golden jackal. Its name belies its scruffy appearance.

[Left] The black-backed jackal looks charming but is a mean scavenger.

A crocodile lies with its mouth agape to control its body temperature.

In or near the water is the crocodile. Often seen basking on the shore when not hungry and waiting for prey, it lies with its mouth wide agape – not, like the hippo, to reveal its fearsome array of teeth, but in order to regulate its body temperature through the skin of its mouth.

Common among the small carnivores are the mongooses, famous for their ability to kill poisonous snakes and ten times less susceptible to snake poison than any other animal of similar size, immortalized by Rudyard Kipling in his story, *Rikki-Tikki-Tavi*, of their Indian counterpart. In Africa there are several species, ranging in size from the large white-tailed mongoose, up to 4 kilos in weight, down to the dwarf mongoose, weighing about 0.25 kilo. Most commonly seen is the banded, of intermediate size. Most are nocturnal, including the marsh mongoose, but the dwarf mongoose is a strictly daylight hunter, living in groups of about 30 and retiring at night into burrows in termite mounds, usually near something like a bees' nest for extra protection. It is said that the hornbill calls down the termite mound holes to wake them up in the morning! In southern Africa we have the meerkat, noted for its communal living and its amusing habit of standing upright on its hind legs to watch for predators. Meerkats differ from other mongooses in that they lack a first toe on all four feet and can close their ears when burrowing.

The phrase 'Nature red in tooth and claw', coined by the poet Alfred Lord Tennyson in 1850, became a byword of the Victorian view of Nature, but in fact life in the wild is not such a bloody battle as may at first appear. If a herbivore in the open spots a predator loping by or lying around it does not flee in terror, but continues with its daily business, albeit keeping a wary eye on the potential danger. If caught by a predator a victim often seems to accept its fate and goes quietly, although some will struggle to the last. But there is no doubt of an animal's fear of predators if it is confined and threatened, as sometimes happens with predators trying to break into a place in which a captive animal has been confined for the night.

[Clockwise from top left]

Banded mongoose.

A dwarf mongoose looks out from its termite mound home.

Meerkats stand completely upright.

Meerkats in characteristic pose.

The nocturnal marsh mongoose.

The hornbill wakes up the dwarf mongoose in the morning.

[Top] These wildebeest keep a wary eye on the lion but do not flee.

[Above] Animals do not flee in panic when they see a lion.

But large mammals do not flee even at the approach of a carnivore, unless it is moving at speed. I have watched a waterbuck buck confront a lion at as little as 30 metres, standing snorting a warning as if daring the lion to attack. On the whole, most animals, although keeping a healthy distance, seem overcome with curiosity at the sight of lions, or conversely ignore them altogether. I have watched a hippo haul itself out of the water in front of a lioness and cubs feeding on a buffalo carcass. It was the lioness that was somewhat nonplussed as the hippo calmly proceeded to graze within a few feet; it was she who kept casting anxious glances at the hippo, not vice versa.

Carnivores do not have the upper hand. If they make a mistake in attack they are not let off lightly, so they needs must exercise skill in capturing their prey. In the bush one day I was fortunate to witness a leopard stalking a warthog; these animals, when adult, weigh approximately the same. The leopard slowly crept to within striking distance. Although out of sight of the warthog it did not leap, and I could see it was waiting for the warthog to face in the other direction. Each time the warthog half-turned away the leopard tensed, muscles bulging, its whole body quivering in anticipation. It was as impatient as I, for suddenly it rushed from cover at the warthog. But it had not waited long enough. The warthog saw it coming and calmly turned to face it. The leopard skidded to a halt some 2 metres away, and sat down. It was an incredible sight. Paws before it like a cat in front of the fire, it sat as if pretending nothing had happened and it was the most normal thing in the world for it to be sitting there. The warthog did not even stop chewing! Facing the leopard, it continued its eating until propriety had been satisfied and it then turned and trotted off. The leopard followed for a few yards, thought the better of it, and gave up. It obviously had great respect for the warthog's tushes and ability to defend itself. Lions, however, have been seen to dig warthogs out of their burrows, even though the warthog always enters its burrow backwards, facing any predator that might come after it.

The predator that has earned the horror of the onlooker is the wild dog, *Lycaon pictus*, the 'painted wolf'. Fitzpatrick described its method of hunting gleaned from native observation back in 1907:

> This, according to the natives, is the system of the wild pack. When they cannot find easy prey in the young, weak or wounded, and are forced by hunger to hunt hard, they first scatter widely over the chosen area where game is located, and then one buck is chosen – the easiest victim, a ewe with young for choice – and cutting it out from the herd, they follow that one and that alone with remorseless invincible persistency. They begin the hunt knowing that it will last for hours – knowing too that in speed they have no chance against the buck – and when the intended victim is cut out from the herd one or two of the dogs – so the natives say – take up the chase and with long easy gallop keep it going, giving no moment's rest for breath; from time to time they give their weird peculiar call and others of the pack – posted afar – head the buck off to turn it back again; the fresh ones then take up the chase, and the first pair drop out to rest and wait, or follow slowly until their chance and turn come round again.

[Clockwise from left]

Spotted hyaena.

Hyaenas prowl at night.

The hunting dog.

But the horror comes from the method of bringing down the prey, for the dogs snatch pieces of flesh from the running animal, aiming for the soft underparts, unlike the big cats, which go for biting the neck, or seizing the muzzle and suffocating it, before consuming the flesh.

Other than the leopard and the cheetah, which hunt alone, other animals such as the lion and spotted hyaena also have co-ordinated methods of hunting. The pack-hunting methods of the spotted hyaena were known in the 19th century, when it was recorded that sickly animals were less likely to be attacked than healthy ones because flight inspired the hyaena to pursue them, whereas the sickly, by standing and facing an aggressor, would deter it from attacking. The hyaena would thus attempt to induce the animal to run before attacking. Referring to 'two or three hyaenas hunting together', it was considered that they would never kill an animal for themselves if they could find a dead one, but the idea that they were solely scavengers seems to be a relatively recent one. In fact, they eat whatever carrion they can find, but also hunt in packs where they are numerous.

The 19th-century explorer Schweinfurth noted that hyaenas hunted fully grown antelopes at night. They do hunt mainly at night, although all prey species are hunted differently, and it seems they may set out to hunt a particular prey regardless of how numerous it is.

Spotted hyaenas are just as efficient at hunting as they are at scavenging, chasing selected prey for up to 3 kilometres at speeds of up to 60 kph, operating in cooperative packs able to pull down an adult buffalo, although the favourite prey is mostly zebra or, where abundant, wildebeest. In southern Africa the gemsbok is usually chosen. Where prey is not abundant there is more scavenging, with about 50 per cent of food consumed being scavenged, but in the Ngorongoro Crater, where wildebeest are abundant, only 10 per cent of food is scavenged. Spotted hyaenas are possessed of large bone-crushing molars, enabling them to crack open and eat bones. They live in clans or associations of family groups, sharing a territory and defending it against those not in the clan. These clans are peculiar in that they are ruled by a female-dominated linear hierarchy: each female is subordinate to the one above it, and the highest-ranking male is subordinate to the lowest female in the line. The young are reared in a den, and when sub-adult some leave the family clan, others stay within it, perhaps for life. Some males become wanderers, others join another clan. The clans range in size from five to eighty depending upon the richness of prey.

There are two other types of hyaena, the brown and the striped. These have rather different lifestyles, and the brown – commonest in the north and south of Africa but less so in the central part – is the grave robber of the ancient writers. The striped hyaena is entirely a scavenger.

Antelopes and gazelles can run faster than lions or leopards, so provided they have warning of an attack can usually escape. The exception over a limited distance is the cheetah, which can run faster than antelopes and gazelles but usually only chooses the latter, which it often catches by cunning manoeuvring rather than in a straight race, causing the victim to swerve or try to double back.

If they become aware of a predator which they detect as a threat, an antelope or gazelle will keep a certain distance from it, known as the 'flight distance'; if this is narrowed it will flee. It may give snorting warning calls to alert others, and some species – gazelles, hartebeest, and

The cheetah can run faster than antelopes and gazelles over short distances.

kob – indulge in a movement known as 'stotting', in which they bounce up and down with all four legs held stiffly, a clear signal to others. In the springbok of South Africa it is known as 'pronking'. It was described in detail by a 19th-century observer:

> the head is lowered almost to the feet, the legs hang fully extended with the hoofs almost brushed together; this arches the back sharply and throws the haunches down, making the legs appear unduly long. In an instant the buck seems to spurn the earth as it shoots up into the air to an incredible height, perhaps straight up; for an instant it hangs arched, then down it drops. … The buck seems scarcely to touch the earth when it bounds into the air again like a rocket, perhaps with a prodigious leap forward and as high as before; for a second you see it in the air, its mane up, its fan raised and opened in a sharp arch, the white patch blazing in the sun and the long hairs glittering, the legs and head all hanging in a bunch under the body; then it touches the earth again, only to bound up once more at a sharp angle to one side, then straight up, then the other side, then forward, and so on.

It is infectious, and soon much of the herd may be pronking, although the activity is short-lived.

Although at one time the lion was popularly referred to as the 'king of the jungle' where 'jungle' was considered to be dense tropical vegetation beset with lianas, as in Kipling's *Jungle Books*, it is in reality open country with scattered trees and bush which is the habitat that the lion favours.

The lion is the largest of the African carnivores, and the most feared by humans, its only real enemy, although a hyaena would attack a sick, injured, or aged lion, and packs of hyaenas have

[Left] Lioness feeding on a wildebeest she has killed.

[Lower left] Leopard. Nocturnal hunters, in quiet places they may spend the day in a tree in full view.

been known to drive lions off their kill. Buffalo are the favourite prey of lion, but the hunters are sometimes seriously injured, even fatally, in taking on such a formidable beast. One lion was seen with blood coming from both ears after such an encounter, and buffaloes have been seen to make determined attempts to flush out lions and attack them. Elephants have been known to kill lions, and lions on a kill will even give way to the ratel if a ratel decides to feed on it.

Lions usually try to kill their prey by getting it on the ground and then suffocating it by biting its throat or holding onto its nose in the case of antelopes; they could not do that easily with a warthog, but they may break its neck. Young lions have been known to take up to 20 minutes to kill a wildebeest, eventually tearing it to pieces. Although lionesses are the principal hunters in a pride, as they usually have a family to feed, those males not attached to a pride perforce do their own hunting. The lucky ones, however, that are attached to a pride move in when the lioness has brought down the prey.

Lions often hunt co-operatively and have been seen to stampede prey into an ambush of other waiting lions; they will also entrap prey by a waterhole or river. Where prey is abundant prides of over 30 members have been encountered, but such large prides are probably cyclical in occurrence; they tend to decline in numbers when conditions such as drought intervene and prey becomes scarcer, or even from the numbers alone leading to infighting among the members. It is considered that although threat is frequent actual fighting is rare, but two lions have been recorded as fighting for ten hours, until one ended up dead, and the other then died of its wounds.

Lions are considered to hunt mainly at night, though at the beginning of the 19th century they were said to hunt mainly during the day but became nocturnal to avoid humans. The leopard, a nocturnal animal, may nevertheless in quiet places spend the day in a tree, in full view.

During the day lions hunt by sight, and some observations suggest they take no notice of wind direction, whilst others only find lions stalking from downwind or through a crosswind. Although the scent of a lion borne on the wind may alert a prey, the latter seems to want to be able to see the lion before fleeing, if it should flee at all. The lions' hunting success rate is believed to be about 5–10 per cent, so the prey has a good chance of escape – unlike from the hunting dog, in which species the hunt has been judged to be 85 per cent successful.

8

Love life, birth, and growing up

As I see it, all organic life is part of a chain reaction to convert energy, which means that animals' lives are solely for the increase of the species. Yet the love life of most of them is very restricted: males are allowed to pair by the females only when the latter are in a state of acceptance dictated by their body chemistry, over which neither party has control, and of which the duration can be very limited. Even then a male must first win his place in society to permit him to pair. Territorial ungulates are sexually mature several years before they have an opportunity to pair, if ever. The young buck waterbuck is capable of reproduction at the age of three, is lucky if he gets a territory by the age of six, and by the time he is ten will probably be ousted by a younger animal and yet may have another eight years to live. But without a territory he usually has no chance of mating. There are exceptions, as illustrated in the photo (page 69); here a lesser kob buck, shown in the extreme right of the photograph, seizes the opportunity to pair with a doe while the dominant bucks are distracted by fighting. This could happen with waterbuck and other territorial animals.

A waterbuck doe, or other antelope, comes into a receptive state for about 24 hours. If pairing is successful at this time she will not be interested again for ten months. Hence when a doe does come into heat, the buck makes the most of it by repeated coupling. Even then the act itself is brief – a matter of seconds in most antelopes. The elephant takes only 15 seconds; in the warthog it is prolonged, and pride of place for endurance goes to the rhino, which requires approximately half an hour to consummate the act.

Most antelopes have a fairly standard pattern of courtship, found in many widely separate groups. Firstly the buck approaches the doe in a characteristic attitude. In the Uganda kob this is with head in the air, in the waterbuck with head down and neck extended. Whatever attitude is adopted, it shows the doe that the buck does not intend to attack her. In preliminary approaches many species, but particularly antelopes and their kind, usually taste the doe's water, its hormone content telling them her reproductive state. Tasting is achieved by the male nuzzling the female from behind causing her to lift her tail and urinate. Antelopes like the waterbuck merely let the urine run over the bare sensory nose patch, but in the giraffe this patch is absent and the bull takes a mouthful then spits it out in a jet. While sampling in this manner, all species curl back their upper lip in a characteristic grimace. Even the black rhino bull does this.

If the interpretation is favourable the buck makes further approaches, and sometimes even if it is not. His next move is that of pawing the doe's hind legs with one of his forelegs, and he may also resort to affectionate rubbing along her flanks or on her back, sometimes reciprocated by the doe. The buck then rises onto her – and more often than not she walks forward, so that he lands on the ground again. This can go on for some time until the doe is completely willing. In his rising excitement the buck, at least in the waterbuck, may try to mount her from any direction. The rump patterns of many antelopes may serve as guides to help prevent this. Certainly they seem to induce mounting responses, for very small calves walking too closely behind their mothers often try to mount them.

When the doe is ready, coupling is the work of a second or two, and the doe immediately walks forward again, so quickly it takes a trained observer to note whether true pairing has taken place. The ancient Roman naturalist Pliny, who lived from 23 to 79 CE, expressed it thus: 'cows and does resent the violence of the bulls and stags and consequently walk forward in pairing'.

After a successful union it may take the doe half an hour to regain her interest in the buck, who recovers first and starts his cajoling again. This process of courting, mating, and resting continues over a day or two, until the heat in the doe has passed.

Lions behave similarly, but the lioness is a little more romantic. The courtship lasts about a week, and she does not walk away during the act but lies snarling, body pressed to the ground. The lion performs the act quickly, after which she rolls over in apparent satisfaction while the lion stands and watches over her until she is ready again. He must be patient, for an unwilling lioness is much more aggressive than an unwilling female ungulate; while the latter passively resists the male's cajoling, the lioness reacts sharply with flailing talons and snapping jaws. The period of heat is long in the lioness and may continue for a week. When she is in heat other males are attracted to her, sometimes coming from many kilometres away, and the original mate may be driven off if he is not powerful enough to keep them away. How do lions at a distance know that a lioness is receptive? Possibly the lioness's courtship odour, or pheromone, is carried long distances in the atmosphere. But I think more likely it is by relayed roaring; a lion answers a lioness, and another lion farther away hears the roar, and so on.

Because of the length of time that it takes, the mating of rhinos has always been a subject of interest, but it was not until the latter part of the 20th century that it was observed in detail. Of course it is not really very different from that of other animals. There are seemingly no long-term preferences in the cow, who accepts the advances of whatever bull is within reach when she comes into heat. The bull first follows her around doggedly wherever she goes. When she stops he shows interest in her, and may indulge in gentle horn play, or give her an affectionate one-and-a-half ton jab in the body. If she seems to like this he rises onto her rump, and remains motionless in this position for long periods until she dislodges him. This can occur many times, and it takes several hours before actual pairing is attempted, when the bull rises onto her rump once more, and drags his brisket into a suitable position. Then the slow, prolonged business, extending up to half an hour, begins, from time to time the cow accompanying the bull's odd stertorous puffings with low squeals.

A feature of rhino pairing is that sometimes the cows violently attack the bull before or after, so he must use all of his wiles to achieve his aim without getting hurt. The motivation of rhinos in playing this game is probably that fear makes the cow attack the bull, until her physiological longing overcomes her resistance.

The Ancient Greek philosopher Aristotle (384–322 BCE), in his book *History of Animals*, did not consider the pairing habits of elephants to be any more spectacular than those of other animals: 'The female', he informed us, 'bends down and divides her legs and the male mounts upon her.' But this was too tame for popular appeal, especially in the Romans, and by the time of Pliny elephants were coupling back to back. Physiologus (circa 200–500 CE), author of the first known bestiary, then squashed it: 'The elephant', the writer categorically stated, 'has no desire to copulate.' Later writers suggested that intercourse must be carried out face to face as the cow's breasts are between her forelegs, in the human position. Her vaginal orifice is also between her back legs, instead of further back, under the tail, as in other animals. The bull's anatomy is peculiar also in that the testes do not descend.

Take a look at an elephant and you will see why its anatomy is arranged in this way. If the cow's breasts were between her back legs like a milch cow's they would drag in the dust, just as would the bull's testes if they were in that position. It may be easy enough to suggest a reason for the position of the elephant bull's testes inside its abdomen, but they pose problems of temperature control, for the testes of other animals are carried externally to keep them below body temperature.

Elephants pair, of course, in the usual position, and speculation otherwise arose simply because the act had not been witnessed. Even today records of elephant mating are rare. In one national park guards of many years' standing said they had never seen it take place. It is a rarer event to witness than in most animals, as the cow pairs only every four to six years. A zoologist friend of mine was lucky after four and a half months' searching to witness the act. Just prior to this, at a scientists' elephant conference held in Uganda's Murchison Falls Park, a pair of elephants obligingly coupled on the hotel patio within feet of the observers. The latter were able to confirm that it follows much the same pattern as in other ungulates.

The cow elephant's heat is brief, lasting for only 24 to 48 hours, and pairing is brief also. It is repeated at frequent intervals during the heat, but differs from some animals in that several different bulls may mount the same cow. As she reaches the peak of her heat, however, the strongest bull keeps the others at bay. During intervals between mounting the bull is kept busy fighting, whilst the cow quietly feeds, indifferent to it all. It is often suggested that the love play includes twining their trunks together, but my observations suggest the contrary; the twining is part of the bull's fighting pattern, wrestling with the trunk to keep an opponent's tusks at trunk's length.

Another animal once thought to pair back to back is the hippo, for the bull's organ is indeed directed backwards. Somehow, however, hippos still manage it in the normal manner, but usually in the water, so we know little about it. Surprisingly enough, even the porcupine

The elephant calf uses its mouth, not its trunk, to suckle.

performs in the same way, variation upon the standard dorsal-ventral position being rare among mammals.

An exception in captivity is the gorilla, which adopts a variety of positions as the whim takes it. In the wild only the customary position has been witnessed, the female crouching on her knees and elbows – but it is performed with somewhat more excitement than by captive gorillas, as they seem to be embarrassed by curious onlookers. In the wild the male roars and the female shrieks, whilst their mating bouts of four to five minutes' duration may be spread over an hour. In his enthusiasm the male has been recorded as pushing the female forward as much as 12 metres. To reach this stage of excitement he requires a lot of arousing, generally showing little interest in sex to begin with. A dominant male is quite unconcerned by younger males sharing the favours of his females. But when a dominant male seems indifferent at first to lesser males pairing with the female, it is believed that these repeated pairings bring the female to a peak, and it is the final dominant male's pairing that is successful in fertilizing the female.

In most animals it is apparent that for the greater part of the time the male's breeding urge is frustrated. Even in seasonal breeders we often find the male is capable of reproduction all the year around. Giraffe bulls often try to mount one another, perhaps as a dominance-asserting role, for giraffes reproduce well. Among baboons and some monkeys, the mounting of each male by another is a gesture of dominance, sexually based but not performed out of a desire to reproduce.

The only real perverts seem to be spotted hyaenas. They are odd enough to start with, as – for us humans at least – it is very difficult to distinguish between the sexes, the bitch having enlarged, male-like external sexual features. Since ancient times it has been alleged that hyaenas change sex from time to time, but this is not true. Nevertheless the males do give vent to strange yelping noises, running around other males excitedly on stiff legs, tails erect, licking one another's genitals, and attempting copulation.

In most species the females, unlike the males, do not suffer from sexual frustration; their behaviour indicates that they have no desire for pairing except when their internal chemistry gets the better of them. This occurs in three-week to one-month cycles in many species if they do not become pregnant; when in heat, though, females may attempt to mount other females, or even a male.

Experience with captive animals suggests that they have erotic zones they can never normally explore in the wild. A buffalo calf of a few months old will go into a complete trance, collapsing on the ground, if its spine is brushed vigorously with a stiff broom! When a year or so of age it still reacts with a glazed expression, but manages to remain standing.

Scratch a warthog or a bushpig on the flank and it will do the same. The eyes become glazed and it falls on to its side, eyes closed in ecstasy. Strangest of all, the hippo likes nothing better than to have its palate rubbed! Force your fingers under its thick, horny upper lip, and it will react by opening its mouth as wide as it can, while you gently rub the roof of its mouth. Don't be afraid; it closes it again slowly, giving you plenty of time to withdraw your hand.

One thing the ancients did not exaggerate was the length of pregnancy of the elephant. Aristotle gave it as two years. In fact it is just over 23 months. Aristotle was pretty accurate when he stated that the cow reaches puberty between 10 and 15 years; work in Africa has shown it to be between 9 and 16 for healthy elephants. But the bull, he considered, attained puberty at 5 or 6 years instead of its actual 8–14.

The length of pregnancy for most species ranges from about six months in small animals such as the duiker, to eight months in the larger antelopes. The hippo takes only eight, but the zebra nearly thirteen. In the rhino it is about eighteen months. It appears that length of gestation is related more to brain size at birth than to body weight.

Many antelopes give birth in solitude, others in company. When the first season's wildebeest calves are born other adults gather round in inquisitive envy, but once calving is in full swing the birth of another individual is too commonplace to elicit any interest. The hartebeest mother on the other hand has a thin time of it: not only does the herd bull do his utmost to prevent her moving away to give birth, but nearby cows attack her when she is in labour. Some animals lie on their side to give birth – whilst one you might most expect it of, the giraffe, remains standing. The baby giraffe falls almost 2 metres into the world and is none the worse for it.

Eating the afterbirth or placenta is a common habit among many species, both herbivore and carnivore, presumably a measure against attracting predators to the spot, but possibly for other reasons too, still the subject of debate. Mobile species like wildebeest and zebra do not bother, whereas hartebeest and waterbuck clean up every trace. The zebra mother makes no

A zebra mare with her newborn foal. She leaves it to get to its feet on its own.

attempt to sever the umbilical cord tying the foal to the placenta. I have watched more than once the difficulty the youngster has escaping from this placental ball and chain. Literally anchored to the ground, the foal struggles back and forth until the cord parts, while the mare simply stands and watches.

The birth of a baby elephant may be attended by 'aunties' who keep intruders at bay and show much concern for the labouring mother. Birth is followed by a long period of attachment of the calf to its mother, as it is not weaned until it is four years old, when the next calf is due. To maintain interest between mother and child for such a long period very strong bonds exist, and the ferocity of a cow elephant defending her offspring is legendary. I once had occasion to assist a park warden destroy a two-year-old calf with a snared foreleg. Cut deeply by the snare and obviously in great pain, it could only keep up with the herd with difficulty, the mother helping it along as best she could. Putting it out of its misery was deemed the kindest solution. A rifle shot bowled it over and instantly the surrounding elephants rushed to its defence. The mother urged it to its feet and, able to get up again, it was hurried into a thicket, where she stood guard while the herd moved away.

Shortly after, however, the calf collapsed and died, at which the distressed mother gave utterance to an eerie penetrating wail of anguish which resounded over the valley. It was a sound that in its haunting dolour and intensity I shall remember all my life, coming so unexpectedly from this great, heartbroken animal. In vain she tried to stand the lifeless calf up, her tusks smeared with its blood. But eventually she accepted the inevitable and wandered dejectedly after the departed herd. A sad tale, but one which demonstrates the extraordinary real feeling and depth of attachment existing between mother and offspring in this species, a necessity to ensure survival where there is such a long period before the young can become independent.

It works the other way round as well, as I discovered when involved in the drugging of a cow elephant to mark her to record her movements (a harmless procedure for the elephant). The selected cow was accompanied by a three-year-old calf, and we waited until the two were on their own, away from the herd, before shooting the dart with its anaesthetizing drug into her. She knew nothing of it, merely collapsing slowly onto the ground, aided by a pull on her tail. We moved in to mark her, thinking the calf would run away. Not a bit of it! When it saw us approach its sleeping mother it made frantic attempts to rouse her, pushing against her with all of its might. This was to no avail, so it turned its attention to us, charging and threatening within a few feet. By dint of dodging around the inert cow and spilling much paint, I managed to paint her ear white despite the calf's protests. The antidote was administered and the cow suddenly got up, quite unaware of what had happened. The calf heaved an almost visible sigh of relief and followed her to catch up with the herd. How frustrating it must have been for it not to be able to tell her what had happened!

The attachment between the parent and young of most other species is probably just as intense, but it is brief. After all, an antelope or zebra can raise four or five offspring in the time it

In the open, elephants form a protective circle around their young.

takes an elephant to raise one. If separated immediately after birth, antelope parents often seem to think nothing more of it. But if they have had time to form a bond, possibly induced by the offspring's first activity of suckling, then it is a different story.

One day, after watching the birth of a waterbuck I tried to capture the calf for marking, but I had waited too long; as I approached in my Land rover, I saw the sudden look of consternation on the mother's face. Her hackles rose, and with hair erect she came stamping and snorting towards me, halting a couple of feet away, daring me to venture closer. Although the doe waterbuck is normally a docile, timid animal, I discovered she can look terrifying if she wants to. I didn't want to be butted in the stomach by 210 kilos of angry antelope, the equivalent of being head-butted by almost three men all at once. My courage failed me and I withdrew for assistance. Shortly afterwards, we separated the two and I managed to mark the calf. Only just in time! As the mother heard its protests she came charging back through the bush. I just managed to leap into the Land rover, whereupon she chased it for more than 50 metres, trying to butt the rear. National parks would be hazardous places if waterbuck does always behaved like this!

Put to the test, many animals will face death to save their young if they have to. I found evidence of this in the zebra. A mare had been killed by lions, and two days later I found her starving foal, almost too weak to move. Its ear and face had been deeply slashed by a lion's claws and it seemed certain the mother had sacrificed herself so that her foal could go free. But despite all our efforts to save it the foal was too far gone, and it died the next day. Commendable as the mother's action may have seemed, it did no good for the species as a whole, as the youngster could not survive alone; but the mare could have produced further offspring had she lived by sacrificing that foal.

The elephant herd protects its young when moving, keeping them hidden within a palisade of pillar-like legs. When lions are scented and the herd has small calves, the adults form a circle with the calves in the centre. The lion likes an elephant calf, and if one strays from the parent it is easy prey. It cannot run fast like an antelope and is helpless until its tusks are of some length, which is not for six years or more. In open country an elephant herd will form a protective circle around the calf if danger threatens, just as the musk-ox of northern Canada does against wolves – but there would be little point in zebra or antelopes trying to do so against lions. There is greater safety in flight, and the long legs of these youngsters are adapted to this end.

This makes them independent creatures at an early age; although they may suckle for six months or more, they do not follow the parent closely. When alarmed they run off, with the parent following or alongside, rather than running to her for protection. How is it that the wildebeest calf can run from birth? First, its stilt-like legs provide it with a long pace with little muscular effort, like a pendulum swinging; a slight movement at the top becomes a wider swing the longer the pendulum. But it has to have energy to use the muscles of its legs, and in the final days before the calf's birth the mother packs in large stores of sugar in the form of glycogen. This rich supply of sugar is stored in the liver of the foetus and in all of its muscles. So the calf does not have to suckle in order to obtain energy; it is already provided. The milk is in fact comparatively weak and is easily digested, as the young of these species can, by accompanying their mother, suckle readily. The young of species such as the buffalo, zebra, topi, and others that follow the parent from birth are similar.

Animals in which this does not happen include the eland, waterbuck, and bushbuck; they are among those species whose young are hidden after birth, resting and growing for three to four weeks before joining the parent and adult groups. In this situation the mother's milk is different, as well. As a dam only visits her baby from time to time she gives a rich milk which is digested slowly.

One animal you would think could defend itself but doesn't is the buffalo. Despite its formidable mien the poor old buffalo is a bag of nerves. Renowned for its ferocity and determination, it is normally one of the most timid of animals. I once surprised an old cow rather suddenly, who got such a fright she fell over, rolling right onto her back, all four legs kicking in the air, before she scrambled to her feet and charged away! Alarm a herd and you are not faced with an impenetrable phalanx of curving horns and menacing bosses, but a retreating, jostling scrummage of naked haunches, tails out, spraying liquid manure over all and sundry, as they disappear into the distance in an apoplexy of fright. Somewhere amongst this dense mass of galloping beasts are the calves, with their unwieldy knobbly legs, valiantly trying to keep up with their elders. Once a herd takes fright like this it goes on for miles. All the ones in front can hear is the thundering of hooves behind them, so they think the danger must still be pursuing them. So the leaders run all the faster, and those behind run the faster to try and keep up, whilst the ones in front become more and more frantic. It can go on like this until the whole herd comes to a halt from sheer exhaustion. In this mad mêlée the cow has little thought for her calf. Once separated in this haunch-to-haunch crush it hasn't much chance of getting back to her side. If such a stampede goes on for long, the youngest calves, of a few days or so, often get left behind in a cloud of dust and bewilderment.

Buffalo flee in panic.

[Left] Elephants are very protective of their calves.

[Lower left] The cheetah mother lets her cubs feed first.

Whatever the bond or association between mother and offspring it lasts usually until the next one is due. Some two or three weeks before the event the parental milk supply dries up and the youngster is on its own, although in some species it will remain with the mother, forming a family group until adult sexual interests break the bond.

Survival of the young is not high in any species. In most, at least 50 per cent of the young, and it may be as high as 75 per cent, die in their first year, from disease, predation, or abandonment.

Lion cubs have to wait to feed until the adults have had their share.

Even the solicitous activities of elephants do not prevent all of their calves being taken by lions. Abandonment is the least likely cause of juvenile mortality, although it sometimes happens to the firstborn. First-time mothers can appear puzzled by their achievement and the pain it may have caused them, and reject the cause of it.

I once rescued a baby hippo born in a native village and abandoned almost immediately by the mother, who had been disturbed by the villagers. Only a few hours old, the youngster gave a good account of itself, trying to charge its tormentors. Eventually, in a rather piedpiperish exit from the village, I got it to a pool. The hippo always gives birth on land, but the youngster is capable of diving almost immediately. This one had never seen water before but when shown the pool it immediately rushed in and submerged, only to come up again blowing and spluttering. Within seconds it had mastered the technique and retired beneath the surface.

If there was not a high mortality among young animals, habitats would soon become overcrowded and there would be insufficient food for all. Carnivores have their own way of maintaining a balance. They give birth to their young in a helpless state, so there is really no comparison between their early period of solicitous care and the more casual link of the ungulates. After mating, a lion stays with his lioness until the cubs are born, although he plays no part in providing for her, and she is usually dependent upon other lionesses, probably siblings, to help provide for the cubs. But once lion cubs are able to follow the mother, she becomes much more indifferent to their needs. Always ready to play with and fondle them, or defend them ferociously from enemies, she is a poor welfare supervisor. When there is not enough food to go around, the cubs go without. At meals they are always kept waiting until last. They must follow the mother wherever she wishes to go, and can drown trying to follow her across rivers. But as a lioness may have six cubs in one year – although three to four is more usual – the land would soon be overrun with lions if there was not a heavy mortality. In the end it balances out. The lower the lion numbers the more food to go round, so the lucky ones get better care. The cheetah is a much better mother and ensures her cubs feed unhindered; but cheetah do not reproduce prolifically, so it is important that as many of their cubs survive as possible.

Before leaving courtship and its consequences I would like to mention one more interesting animal, the crocodile. Crocodiles pair in the water, and the bull indicates his intentions by joyful splashing, arching his tail, and opening his mouth. Once he has singled out the cow of his choice the pair then swim in circles, the cow lifting her snout from time to time and grunting.

The varanid lizard preys on crocodile eggs.

The crocodile has existed for 190 million years.

Sidling up to her, the bull cautiously places a foreleg on her shoulder. If this meets with no resistance he pulls her to him, and climbs onto her. Pairing is effected in a half dorsal-ventral, half ventral-ventral position, the bull twisting his tail end over to bring the genital regions into contact. The act, longer than most, lasts for just under a minute. At night the cow retires to the shore. Here she scrapes out a nest, laying in it two to four dozen white, goose-size eggs, which she then carefully covers over. Then follows a long four-month vigil guarding the nest, although she does not actually brood. Her task is to keep away the hungry birds and monitor lizards that like nothing better than a meal of crocodile eggs.

At last, after this long incubation, the young are ready to emerge. Still inside the egg they grunt vigorously in response to any nearby disturbance, such as tapping on the ground. This is to let the parent know they are ready to be let out. As they are incapable of emerging by themselves, the mother must dig them up and release them from the shell, whereupon they scuttle for cover to avoid the goliath herons, marabou storks, and monitor lizards, all waiting for a meal. These baby crocs do not seem to like being introduced to water straightaway. When they are ready it appears the mother carries them there, riding on her back and snout. She then establishes a nursery in the shallows from which they eventually disperse. At this stage they eat aquatic insects.

Until the vogue in crocodile-skin handbags destroyed their numbers, this method of reproduction, hazardous as it may appear with its long incubation period and the many hungry predators to contend with, had kept the crocodile a highly successful animal for 190 million years.

9

The wanderers —
migration and irruption

Every year in Africa, passing unnoticed by most, a remarkable phenomenon takes place. This is the influx from Europe of some 50 different species of migratory birds, all hastening south to avoid the unfriendly northern winter. Many, such as the nightingale, which we consider typically a part of the English countryside, spend just as much time in Africa as they do in England.

The cuckoo, whose first call in England each year creates so much excitement in the newspaper columns, is just as much at home on the African savannah as it is in an English woodland. This introductory call heralds the first travel-stained migrants to have completed the two-month journey.

During the English autumn swallows lined up in serried ranks on the telephone wires used to be a common sight, although less so today. But by the time they have reached Africa their ranks have become dispersed and few people notice their arrival. We know, however, that those that winter in Uganda are mainly from Germany and Scandinavia, whilst British swallows carry on to the Cape. This much has been learnt from ringing. Apart from such legitimate marking methods, the European storks – well known on the Continent, where they were mythically regarded as the bringer of babies, but rarely seen in England – sometimes come back north with arrows sticking through them. In some cases it has been possible to identify the areas the storks have passed through in Africa from the particular type of arrow, or even the hunter's personal identification marks on it. I saw one of these unfortunate birds in the Serengeti National Park before it made its journey north, or tried to. Although their numbers have now diminished, an estimated 170,000 formerly travelled down the eastern side of Africa each year, where they are called the locust bird from their habit of preceding locust swarms. Flying ahead, they settle and wait for the locusts to descend on them. Having gorged they fly ahead and wait again. Concern has been expressed in Europe at the decline in numbers of this stork. Could it be that the highly

[Left] Side-striped jackal with a stork it has killed in the Serengeti.

[Below] An Abdim's stork on the right, a migrant within Africa, with a yellow-billed stork on the left.

Locust birds in Tanzania which migrate to and from Europe and Africa.

successful campaign waged against locusts in Africa has deprived the bird of one of its most important foods?

Martins, swifts, swallows, kites, falcons, waders, ducks, storks, tiny willow-wrens, and many other birds, too, converge upon Africa from as far away as Siberia, often residing from October to March, throughout the breeding period of the resident birds. Some of the wanderers never bother to go back home again. A pair of swallows lived under the eaves of my veranda in the Akagera National Park, Rwanda, during the entire 18 months that I was there, and had obviously been there for some time before I arrived. They did not rear any young; perhaps that may have meant they lacked the migratory impulse.

Migrations also take place within Africa. Due to the regular alternation of wet and dry seasons either side of the equator, more regular seasonal movements of birds occur within East Africa than in any other such region in the world. The nondescript Abdim's stork nests during the wet seasons between May and September in a band north of the equatorial rainforest, stretching from the west coast to the Red Sea. At the end of the rains it flies south, passing through Kenya and Uganda, and spends the next few months in Tanzania and most of southern Africa, returning in February. The standard-winged nightjar breeds in the dry season, in a belt stretching from Senegal to Kenya along the edge of the tropical rainforest. In the wet season it moves north and its place is taken by the plain nightjar, which behaves in roughly the opposite manner. Where their ranges coincide they operate a sort of shuttle service. The nightjars are careful not to tread on one another's toes, so how do all of these other outside invaders manage to fit in? The total number of migratory species equals only one thirtieth of the total African species, but the barn swallow, for instance, far outnumbers the native African swallows. It is remarkable, amongst such notoriously territorial animals, that these migrants can fit in and compete with residents presumably better adapted to local conditions than they are.

Among mammals the situation is simpler, as the migratory route is usually circular and the species involved are not replaced by other species when they are not in residence in a particular area.

The best-known migratory animal in East Africa is the Serengeti wildebeest. Its vast herds of over 5,000, totalling at one time 1.3 million animals altogether, have created more attention than the bird migrations. The causes of the migration are probably the same, the animals seeking better feeding areas and places suitable for rearing young. But the Serengeti wildebeests' movements are continuous, as opposed to the abrupt journeyings of migratory birds, and neither are they fraught with the hazards bird migrants face; for the wildebeest the greatest hazard is when it comes to crossing rivers, when many often drown, trampled under the surface by the pressing hordes behind them, or are taken by crocodiles. Carnivores follow the migratory herds, but take their normal toll; their activities are best termed nomadic, though, rather than migratory, as they follow wherever their prey leads them.

Far to the south, 3,000 kilometres away at the other end of Africa, vast herds of wildebeest also occur, but also hartebeest and eland, undergoing migration in the Kalahari Desert. The numbers of wildebeest are not as great as in the Serengeti, perhaps reaching a little over a quarter of a million in good years, because, due to its aridity, the Kalahari is only a tenth as productive as the Serengeti, with an average of less than a quarter of the rainfall and prone to drought in roughly 20-year cycles. But it is not as desert as the Sahara, its 5–10 cm of rain a year allowing a thin cover of grass and stunted thorny bush. After a run of good years the animal numbers build up, and then, when the cyclical drought conditions return, the herds are forced to migrate in search of water. Moving north, west, and south as they migrate in their search, their numbers are swelled by others along the route in a domino effect, for the intruders, in ever-increasing numbers, eat what is left to eat of the dry vegetation, so those animals which were subsisting on it are forced to move on with the crowd in search of better pastures. If the water they seek has dried up, then they die in vast numbers, not only from thirst, but because their hordes eat everything around them. Thus it has seemingly always been since this cyclical drought pattern was established, although the numbers do not now reach their historic proportions. Those few animals, about 10 per cent of the whole, which somehow survive until the rains come, then drift back to their original home areas. So this is a very different migration pattern from that in the Serengeti.

Elephants probably once migrated long distances, but today most of their routes have been severed by settlement, restricting the elephants to smaller and smaller areas. Unable to move out in search of food, they are forced, by virtue of their numbers, to destroy their own habitat. Before poaching devastated their numbers this was happening in national parks throughout eastern and southern Africa.

A hundred years ago many more mammals migrated in East Africa – thousands of animals such as zebra and Tommy in the Rift Valley – but as there are only scattered remnants of these once great herds, they no longer have any need to search far for food, even if they could pass the fences and farmlands that now block their paths.

[Left] A stream full of catfish migrating to spawn in the Akagera Park, Rwanda.

[Below] Catfish massed together in their thousands.

Catfish leaping like a salmon.

Some of the best-known migratory habits are those of fish, made famous by stories such as Henry Williamson's *Salar the Salmon*. Although its habits are not as well known as those of the salmon, the African catfish, *Clarias mossambicus*, is the most remarkable of the African anadromous fishes, those that migrate against the current to spawn. Unprepossessing with its large flat head and wide ugly mouth beset with barbels, it leaves the main rivers at the onset of the first heavy rains, usually in February to March. Surging up the small flood channels and tributaries swollen with the rains, it is in a hurry. It must lay its eggs in time for them to hatch and the young to be able to follow the adults back to the rivers again before the swamps and tributaries dry up. Many adults and young never manage to make this return journey, and then the fish eagles, marabou storks, and vultures have a grand feast, helping themselves to the catfish trapped in their hundreds in the mud of dwindling pools on a flood plain or along some temporary river bed.

I was lucky to witness a migration in Rwanda's Akagera National Park early one February, when conditions brought them upstream all at once. A relatively shallow swamp meandering through the rushes was suddenly jammed with thousands upon countless thousands of writhing catfish. The water boiled with them, and above the constant roar like a waterfall that their splashing produced, I could even hear some grunting. My vantage point was a causeway and some of them, like salmon, repeatedly flung themselves out of the water against the rocks, only to fall back and try again. Others, impatient in the vast queue to pass through the small channels in the causeway, searched the side ditches, wriggling over land if needs be. Finding a dead end, they had to wriggle all the way back again. The fish eagles took their fill, and the massed spectacle continued for several days until, just as suddenly as it had all begun, the swamp was quiet again. I had a similar encounter with catfish in the north of the Central African Republic where, camped one night by a small rivulet, I was awakened after dark by the sound of rustling in the grass to find numerous catfish wriggling on land from the water. Where they were trying to go to I did not determine.

Migration implies a return journey, whether the animal achieves it or not. Apart from a few butterflies, most insects are not migratory, even the most famous example of all, the migratory locust. Locusts take a one-way ticket, so their movements are irruptions (bursting out), rather than migrations.

Irruptions result from population build-ups due to a succession of favourable factors – or, conversely, unfavourable ones. When this occurs to the degree that the original home cannot support all the numbers, almost the whole population emigrates. This is more characteristic of poor areas, like semi-deserts, where the animals are usually kept low in numbers by lack of food but have a tremendous potential for increase if the right conditions come along. In well-balanced habitats like central Africa, where there are too many hungry predators, parasites, and diseases ready to fling themselves upon the easy source of food provided by irruptions, such build-ups seldom have a chance to develop – but locust irruptions have been known since biblical times. Several locust species live in East Africa, the main pest being the red locust, *Nomadacris septemfasciata*. This is just a very large, fat, grasshopper, some 7.5 cm long. Its main home is the Rukwa Valley in southwest Tanzania, an arm of the Eastern Rift occupied by a lake 145 kilometres long and 24 kilometres wide. The surrounding plain, which is subject to extreme variations of flooding and drying, is said to be one of the finest bird haunts in Africa, as well as having large herds of buffalo, topi, zebra, and other game. Among this profusion of life can be found the red locust, normally living its life just like any other grasshopper. But every so often the pattern of flooding and drying of the plain produces favourable conditions for the locusts' increase, and their numbers start to race away from what's left after the toll taken by countless birds and other enemies.

When the numbers reach a certain density the locusts start to cluster together, and at that point even their colour and pattern has changed. They are now known as gregarious locusts, and have become the start of a menace. Soon they fly off in great swarms, estimated at times to consist of up to 1,000 million individuals, each with a capacious appetite for green food. The swarms may be as much as an astonishing 30–65 kilometres long, and from 3–8 kilometres wide, and they can travel for eight months. In November and December their journey is halted for egg-laying. The swarm comes to rest and the females deposit their eggs in the soil, each laying about 70. When this is accomplished the swarm flies on. Halting two weeks later, it repeats the process. And so it continues until each female has laid about 300 eggs. If conditions are favourable, about one month after the first batch has been laid, the eggs hatch. This is followed at fortnightly intervals by the other batches all along the route of the parent swarm.

Emerging from the soil the newly-hatched locusts, unable to fly, are known as hoppers. Joining together they begin to hop on their journey for food. Where they cross railway lines their thousands of crushed bodies bring trains to a halt on the slippery rails. Where they enter the farmers' fields not a blade of green foliage is left. For two to three months they continue their devastating journey of havoc. But all the time the predators, parasites, and diseases are building up their onslaught, relentlessly whittling away at the hopping hordes. The hopper cannot become an adult with wings until it has moulted six times, and a lot can happen to it before that is achieved. After the sixth moult, however, it can fly, and repeat the cycle all over again.

Once a frequent menace to native agriculture, the locust has now largely been brought under control by attacking it at its permanent breeding sites. Locusts are eaten eagerly by many Africans, but more favoured in parts of Uganda is the long-horned grasshopper they call *nsenene*, *Homorocoryphus nitidulus*, a slender green insect which swarms at the end of the rains. Unlike the locust it is a nocturnal flier and so is attracted to lights, particularly the street lights of Kampala where large numbers can bring traffic to a halt with their crushed and slippery bodies on the road. *Nsenene* is eaten fried, and although friends of mine have tasted it, I cannot vouch for their approval.

Recently revealed is the remarkable migration of the painted lady butterfly, *Vanessa cardui*, which graces English gardens in the summer, coming from Europe to breed. Found on every continent except South America, and widespread in Africa, the British visitor was formerly thought to die when winter approaches, but has now been found to undergo a remarkable southerly migration to the desert fringes of North Africa. Flying high in the sky at about 500 metres, sometimes reaching heights of over 1,000, it covers a round trip of over 14,000 kilometres, some individuals even going north to the Arctic Circle. But the butterfly that packs its bags and leaves Britain is not the same individual that returns; it can take up to six generations to complete the circular tour. Think of this remarkable journey to be undertaken when you next see this pretty butterfly in an English garden. In distance travelled it outranks the milkweed butterfly, *Danaus chryssipus*, known for its long migrations in America. In Africa the milkweed is known as the African queen or monarch; migrating within Africa it is widespread, and being toxic to predators is mimicked by a number of other butterflies.

Several species of butterfly migrate seasonally within Africa. One of the commonest in South Africa, the brown-veined white *Belenois aurota*, migrates annually from the west coast of South Africa in a north-east direction, laying eggs, like locusts, along the route, and moving in clouds up to a kilometre high, to descend on Madagascar. Such movements occur elsewhere in Africa.

Another insect irrupting in incredible numbers is a little fly known simply as the lake fly, *Chaoborus edulis*. The causes of its irruptions differ from those of the locust, as they are regular and result from all of the flies emerging from the larval state at once. The larva is an aquatic inhabitant of the larger East African lakes such as Victoria and Edward. Once each month, just after the new moon, batches of larvae emerge as adults, bursting out of the surface of the lake like the more familiar mayfly of British waters. So great is their number that the batches look like a pall of black smoke rising for hundreds of metres into the sky above the water. Fortunately for all concerned, these fantastic swarms usually expend themselves in the lake. Like mayflies, unable to feed, the flies live for just a few hours to pair. But if the wind is in the wrong direction these nuptial swarms may be blown off the water to cover the land like

The *Mormyrus* or elephant-snout fish.

a yellow pea-soup fog. Smaller than mosquitoes, lake flies find their way through the smallest fly mesh and have horrified many an American tourist returning to their lakeside hotel room after supper. But they have no mouthparts and are quite harmless, unless you become trapped in the centre of a swarm when their sheer numbers could choke you to death – a fate said to occasionally befall local fishermen.

Although in its larval state it is the most numerous insect of the big lakes it is seldom fed upon by a fish that makes larvae its business. This is the peculiar-looking elephant-snout fish, *Mormyrus kannume*, which has a long, down-curving snout that it pokes into the bottom mud like a vacuum cleaner, sucking up small aquatic creatures. The Chaoborus larva spends most of its life in the plankton, the rich soup of diatoms, algae, and small creatures that floats near to the surface. It only sinks to the bottom in its final stage of aquatic life, living in the mud by day and swimming up to the surface at night. As the elephant-snout fish is a nocturnal feeder, it misses this rich source of food almost entirely.

There are others beside insects that irrupt. In Africa, birds irrupt too. A pretty little red-billed weaver, the Sudan dioch or quelea, builds its numbers into such millions that it becomes a serious grain pest in parts of Africa. So great are its numbers that outright warfare with bombs and flame-throwers is waged against it. In Tanzania over 500,000,000 were estimated to have been killed at one period, yet humans still did not get the upper hand. The birds descend in vast cheeping clouds to devour whole fields of wheat, presenting to the farmer a greater threat than the locust. Normally the quelea is no more of a threat than any other type of weaverbird, until conditions spark off these vast increases, aided and abetted by farmers providing rich sources of easily obtainable food.

Until the last great outbreak in 1893, springbok underwent tremendous population increases, trekking in vast massed numbers.

Irruptions among mammals in Africa are few, but we have the notable exception of the South African springbok, a strange gazelle separated from those of East Africa by a band of over 1,600 kilometres in which no gazelles occur. Until the last record in 1893, the springbok had undergone a tremendous population increases aided by good conditions, but when drought came and the food supply was exhausted, there resulted a blind, unstoppable pilgrimage, which, like those of the lemmings of northern climes, often ended in the sea. So dense were the numbers that they are said to have trampled to death everything in their path. The Dutch farmers used to turn out and slaughter them until they were exhausted from the effort, but still the hordes pressed on unchecked. Presumably only when sufficient had died and the numbers had thinned or rain had scattered them did the frenzy subside and the survivors settle down to normal life once more.

The springbok was a remarkable exception – its numbers are now too low for a recurrence of this habit, as their numbers do not have time to build up to such levels before drought cuts them down again – for mammal irruptions are usually confined to smaller species, rodents in particular, which produce more than one offspring at a time and have short intervals between litters. From time to time Tanzania is witness to build-ups of a creature known as the multimammate rat, which has several pairs of teats to accommodate its large litters. When breeding is favourable it produces larger litters, and grows even more teats.

10

Curiouser and curiouser

The stranger side of African natural history would not be complete without including some very specialized creatures – the parasites. Early hunters expressed surprise at the numbers of these creatures they found both outside and inside the animals they had shot. When introduced livestock died of disease the belief developed that African animals were particularly prone to parasitism and so infected the livestock. In fact most parasites found in Africa are found elsewhere in the world, and such parasite loads would not have been unfamiliar to farmers almost anywhere at that time.

Lice occur on African hyraces and English dormice; lungworms infest zebras and porpoises; trypanosomes turn up in antelopes in Africa and in deer in the Arctic circle (the first trypanosome to be discovered was in a trout). Two centuries ago one could catch malaria in Epping Forest. I would even hesitate to say that parasites are more numerous in Africa than elsewhere. Their striking feature is their variety, but considering the variety of hosts even this is not surprising.

An animal in normal health has no difficulty in supporting its associated parasites, supplying them with food it can spare. But when an animal becomes weakened by drought, starvation, or wounds, then the parasites whittle away reserves the animal can ill afford to part with. In 1926, Charles Elton, in his book *Animal Ecology*, succinctly defined the difference between a parasite and a carnivore: whereas the former exists on income, the latter lives off capital.

A parasite is not necessarily attached to its host. The most infamous of all African parasites, the tsetse fly, merely swoops from a bush onto a passing animal, takes a blood meal, and then dives back into its resting place. Playing a minor role in the host's natural life, the tsetse fly has become both scourge and saviour of African wild life; few wild animals would be left in many parts of Africa today if it was not for its presence in those places, keeping out humans and cattle.

A tsetse fly looks much like its relative the common house fly, except that when at rest it folds its wings over its back in scissor-fashion, and instead of laying eggs it gives birth to a single offspring as a fully-grown larva. This immediately pupates, to later emerge as an adult. Each time a female fly wishes to produce an offspring she must first take a blood meal. It is in doing this that she may transmit another parasite, an internal one. This is the trypanosome, a microscopic blood parasite, some species of which are fatal to humans or cattle. That which causes the fatal cattle disease *nagana* is Bruce's trypanosome, *Trypanosoma brucei*. It has been found in buffalo, wildebeest, duiker, reedbuck, waterbuck, steenbuck, bushbuck, eland, kudu, sitatunga, impala, hartebeest, warthog, and spotted hyaena.

Sleeping sickness, a disease fatal to humans, is caused by variations of Bruce's trypanosome, the Rhodesian trypanosome the deadliest, and the Gambian trypanosome which works its evil more slowly. But other than a single isolation of the Rhodesian trypanosome from a bushbuck in more than a century of research, there is only suggestive evidence that these harmful trypanosomes are harboured by wild ungulates. Nonetheless a decision was taken over a century ago that if all the wild animals in Africa were destroyed, the tsetse fly, deprived of food, would starve to death. This policy was pursued relentlessly, despite the findings of research that the method was not effective. As might be expected, the flies found alternative sources of food, particularly livestock.

There are eleven species of tsetse fly in East Africa, but not all feed on humans or cattle. They have definite preferences, so it is certainly not necessary to kill every animal, even if the killing of any could be justified. In a part of Tanzania it was found that rhino and buffalo were the favourite hosts of one fly, whilst the more numerous animals inhabiting the area – kongoni, impala, and Grant's gazelle – were not fed upon by the fly at all. In another place it preferred nocturnal animals such as porcupine, antbear, and small cats, ignoring waterbuck and impala. The waterbuck is one of the animals most heavily infected by trypanosomes, yet is least favoured by any tsetse fly.

The favourite hosts of the tsetse *Glossina palpalis* (*Glossina*, 'tongued', because of the fly's protruding mouthparts with which it stabs its victim, hence loosely 'the tongued fly', and *palpalis*, 'feeler', thus the 'tongued feeler fly') are crocodile, monitor lizard, and tortoises. The tongued fly will as a last resort bite humans, and is believed to have been responsible for the great 1909 sleeping sickness epidemic in Uganda. Hence it was proposed that all of the crocodiles in Lake Victoria should be destroyed (nobody thought about the lizards and tortoises), an idea fortunately not put into practice, although poachers have since almost completed the task.

Wild animals carry many trypanosomes that have no effect upon man or cattle. The waterbuck seems to be most heavily infected, followed by kudu, reedbuck, giraffe, bushbuck, and eland. Others are less so, the zebra rarely, and some animals not at all. Trypanosomes are common in many animals outside of Africa.

Other biting flies besides tsetses annoy wild animals. I have watched resting waterbuck at night leap up and gallop madly away to shake off the attentions of mosquitoes. The large horseflies, tabanids, can be over an inch long with a proboscis like a large hypodermic needle and a sting to match. At the other extreme a tiny fly of the water's edge merely drives one frantic with its tiny bites delivered en masse. This is a particular type of blackfly, *Simuliidae*, of which 57 species live in Africa and some species of which occur as far north as the Arctic Circle. It breeds in swift-flowing streams, up to nearly 4,200 metres in altitude on Mounts

[Above] Botflies on the hide of a rhino.

[Left] The rhino botfly parasite, wingspan 6.4 cm.

[Below] An elephant foot maggot at home in an elephant's foot.

Kenya and Kilimanjaro. The aquatic larvae live attached to stones and weeds, and some to the carapace of freshwater crabs. Like tsetses they are harmful for what they transmit, in this case a microscopic creature known as a filariid worm. One such worm lives in the tear gland of the buffalo, causing irritation such that the animal will rub bare patches in front of its eyes. This can be easily seen on buffaloes in Uganda.

It is nice to know that there are some flies that cannot bite at all. These have peculiar life histories with the larval stage spent inside a mammalian host. Such a fly is the rhino bot, *Gyrostigma rhinocerontis*. Its 6 cm or more wingspan makes it the largest fly species known in Africa, and it must also be the largest free-living invertebrate parasite. A smaller species parasitizes the zebra, laying its eggs on the hairs of the mane and fetlocks, even on those of newborn foals. When the animal grooms it takes in some of these eggs, which then hatch in the stomach. Here the larvae live attached to the stomach wall, eventually passing through the gut to emerge and pupate on the ground. The rhino species lays its eggs at the base of the horn and in folds of skin, and the larvae, when they hatch, bore into the skin rather than being ingested. When cattle hear the buzz of the allied oestrus or warble fly approaching them to lay its eggs – to produce bots just like the rhino bot, except that the grubs live under the skin – they are driven frantic by the sound, but the rhino seems unperturbed by their presence.

When the black rhino becomes extinct this remarkable parasite will go with it. A report stated that despite the near-extinction of the rhino the numbers of the fly were thriving. I have no doubt that the apparent increase in the fly is in fact because the fewer the individual hosts available the more the bot flies have to crowd onto the remaining few; but over-infestation may cause the rhinos to sicken.

A most curious variant lives in the soles of elephants' feet, where its home is a little tunnel it makes through the thick horny pad to the outside world. I was fortunate to be able to take probably the first pictures of this parasite, *Neocuterebra*, actually at home in an elephant's foot. Also curious is its relative, *Pharyngobolus*, whose larvae crawl up the inside of the elephant's trunk to live attached to the oesophagus.

The warble flies mentioned above are well known to sheep and cattle farmers in Africa, and allied species occur in some antelopes. The adult fly lays its eggs on the host's skin or hair, and when the eggs hatch the larvae bore into the skin. They live in various parts of the body, eventually coming to lie just under the skin of the back, breathing through a small hole that they make. The pied crow considers them a great delicacy and pecks them out if the host is willing. Warble flies occur on Grant's gazelle in East Africa, and I have seen them causing bumps on the skin of the steenbok in Botswana.

Other botflies, known as oestrids, and equally unpleasant, live in the nostrils of their victims. The violent sneezing of wildebeest or hartebeest that you often see is the animal sneezing out the larvae which are ready to pupate. They occur also in warthogs and even in hippos.

If these life histories seem strange, then those of the liver flukes are even more so. The eggs of a liver fluke are passed in the host's droppings and must be eaten by a certain water snail, not any old snail. Inside the correct snail they hatch and pass through several larval stages before literally bursting out. They now have a little tail that they use to propel themselves up stems of

Sharp's grysbok in Botswana. They are infected by warble flies.

wet grass. The larvae then build a hard covering around themselves and rest within their casing or encyst. In this state they remain imprisoned until eaten by an unlucky antelope or hippo. If eaten by the right host they are not digested but emerge from their little prison and travel to the liver. Here, in the hippo, the fluke grows to nearly more than 10 cm in length and starts the cycle all over again.

The hippo plays host to another strange parasite allied to the fluke. This is a flatworm or trematode, *Oculotrema hippopotami*, which lives on the surface of the hippo's eyeball. Until not so many years ago this parasite was known from only a single specimen found on a hippo in 1924 in Cairo Zoo. In fact it is so common in the wild that you can actually see the worms crawling about when the hippo blinks its eye, causing froth around the eyelids. The hippo likes nothing better than for someone to rub the cornea of its eye as hard as possible to relieve the irritation!

In some waters hippo are groomed by at least four types of fish: a carp of the genus *Labeo* hoovers up algae from the skin, a little cichlid cleans the dung from the bristles on the tail, an African barbel cleans the soles of its feet and between the toes, and a small fish of the genus *Garra*, known as the doctor fish, nibbles at wounds, removing dead skin – but it is believed that they may also eat flesh, preventing healing. Nevertheless, the hippos seem to like these attentions.

Best-known of all internal parasites is the tapeworm. Many live in African animals, although the longest of all lives in the human gut. In 'wild' tapeworms the final stages are passed in almost all herbivores, whilst the intermediate stages occur in carnivores, particularly the lion. But a peculiar type inhabiting the zebra passes this intermediate stage in rather a small carnivore – a mite. The mite eats the eggs it finds on the ground in the zebra's droppings, and these hatch inside it. The larva that emerges promptly encysts in the mite and no further development takes place unless the mite is eaten by a zebra. Then the tapeworm is released and attaches itself to the zebra's gut wall for the rest of its life.

The chances of many of these parasites surviving to adulthood cannot be far different from you or me winning a fortune on the lottery. Particularly is this true of the 'hard' tick, nonetheless one of the most familiar of external parasites. Ticks abound in the African grasslands in millions but only a small percentage reach a host. So they must be tremendously prolific, and a female lays 3,000–10,000 eggs. Only two of these eggs need to reach maturity to keep the population numbers constant. After such prodigious effort the female dies. The male has succumbed already after the single act of mating. Like the tsetse fly, the female tick must gorge on blood before she can produce any eggs. This done she drops to the ground and lays her eggs in the soil. Here they hatch into microscopic six-legged larvae known as pepper ticks. They immediately climb a grass stalk and crowd at the top to await a passing victim. Anyone unlucky enough to brush against one of these voracious queues is covered with a swarm of these irritating creatures. If they attach to an appropriate host they feed for several days then drop off and moult; as they can only stretch their skin a little they have to shed it to reveal a fresh, soft skin underneath. Their chances of attaining maturity have now been increased by a third. Having shed their old skin they emerge in their new soft skin as nymphs, now with eight legs. Again the wait at the top of a grass stalk must take place, followed for the lucky ones by an encounter with a host, then feeding and stretching the skin to its utmost, and then shedding the skin again. This time they emerge as adults, and the final phase of their precarious life history is entered.

The adult mounts a grass stalk for the last time and begins its patient wait. Should an animal brush past the tick may make a desperate leap onto it and plunge its serrated proboscis into the animal's skin. But ticks have preferences, and the fate of those that attach to the wrong host is unknown. Do they simply die? Or do they drop off and try again? The individual's chances of reaching maturity are remote, but they are aided by an extraordinary tenacity of life. Some adults have been kept unfed, yet alive, in the laboratory for five years.

Ticks occur on almost all African animals, even under the scales of snakes. The hippo has its own species, which lives around its ears, managing to survive a continual dousing with water. Buffalo carry large numbers, although we have only a vague idea of what 'large numbers' might mean. I have found 5,000 not unusual on a healthy waterbuck.

Another type, the 'soft' tick, is, fortunately, much less common. It is found only on burrowing hairless animals like aardvark and warthog. Not having such a precarious method of finding a host it lays fewer eggs and its population numbers are much smaller. Both types of tick transmit several blood diseases harmful to both humans and cattle, but their effects upon their wild hosts are unknown.

The louse is one of the more interesting ectoparasites (as we call those that live on the outside of an animal, as against endoparasites, which live inside). The louse comes in three types, the most common those which feed on scurf and skin debris. Then there are the bloodsuckers, and an intermediate form found only on warthog and elephant. Two species live only on warthog, and a third on both African and Asian elephants. Lice are interesting because they are so conservative in their choice of host, preferring death to life on the wrong animal.

Apes and monkeys are often called lousy animals but in the wild this is far from being the case, for their continual grooming keeps them remarkably free of lice. Pride of place for lousiness goes to the hyrax, with over twenty-five different species to its credit. The evolution of the hyrax seems to have been so slow that its lice have evolved faster than the host, a reversal of the usual situation, lice generally lagging behind the evolution of their hosts.

I have found no more than 500 on a waterbuck, but up to 5,000 have been recorded on a Uganda kob. The numbers on any wild animal are dwarfed by those that can be found on humans. When Thomas Becket lay murdered in Canterbury Cathedral observers reported that his clothing looked as if it was boiling, caused by the movement of the vast numbers of lice spurred into action by his cooling body.

Perhaps the most unpleasant parasite is a little mite, *Raillietia*, which lives in the ears of waterbuck and kob, and some other animals. Its crawling causes such an irritating tickling sensation that in some places almost every adult animal carries large scabs under its ears from continual scratching. Old waterbuck become so frantic in their efforts to rid themselves of this annoyance that the whole side of the face may be rubbed bare. Altogether eight species are known, the most common being ubiquitous in cattle, with recently two new ones found in Brazil. Another common species is found in goats. For many years, apart from the cattle and waterbuck species, this mite had only been recorded elsewhere in the Australian wombat!

Although the body itself fights parasites to some extent, the hosts cannot consciously do much about their internal ones. Suggestions that they eat certain herbs and grasses, and visit salt-licks for this purpose, are questionable. But an animal can take positive action against its ectoparasites, and many resort to dust and mud baths to relieve the irritation. Hairless animals like elephant, rhino, and warthog love to wallow, but antelopes seldom resort to this. Perhaps they are cleverer at grooming themselves. Mammals are aided in their battle by certain birds; the best-known association is the rhino and its tick birds, *Buphagus*, a type of starling, the red-billed and the yellow-billed oxpeckers, although these birds will groom almost any large mammal that will let them. Two that object are the waterbuck and the elephant. I knew an old grey doe waterbuck that was always the one to be singled out by tick birds, but as soon as they settled on her she would gallop around furiously to shake them off. Most animals welcome their attentions, and stand with a bemused look while the birds probe their most ticklish parts. The yellow-billed oxpecker occurs mostly in West Africa, more restricted in its range in East Africa than the red-billed, which is a partial migrant up and down the eastern side of Africa. Intimately adapted to their hosts with modified claws and beak, they even use their hosts' hair for nest lining. They are said to have a symbiotic, or mutually beneficial, association with the black rhino, as they fly off noisily if approached, alerting the rhino.

Although the elephant seems to object to the tick bird, for some reason it does not object to the piapiac, *Ptilostomus afer*, a type of crow found in northern Uganda. Primarily a West African species that extends across to western and northern Uganda, the piapiac is a noisy, jet black bird, which hunts for insects on the ground in large, cheeky, chattering flocks, turning

[From top]

Black rhinoceros with its attendant red-billed oxpeckers giving the alarm by flying off.

Buffalo with attendant egrets, which wait for insects to be disturbed by it.

White rhino with piapiac birds.

[Left] A giant rat.

[Right] *Hemimerus talpoides*, a flightless earwig which lives on the giant rat.

its attention to any large mammal that happens along. In the Murchison Falls National Park it quickly accustomed itself to the white rhinoceros when it was introduced there, albeit that in the event its introduction was short-lived due to poachers.

Another example of the more casual relationship is the buff-backed heron or cattle egret, *Bubulcus ibis*, a small white stork-like bird with a yellow bill, equally at home catching frogs in a swamp or picking ticks off a buffalo's belly.

It is nice to know there are some associations of mutual benefit. If the creature does not feed on the host but on its waste products such as scurf, it is known as a commensal. One of the most bizarre of such associations is that existing between the giant rat and a degenerate earwig, blind and wingless. Known by the name of *Hemimerus talpoides*, it lives permanently on the rat's body, moving through the hair on its side, feeding on scurf and fungus spores. Unlike other earwigs it does not lay eggs but produces live young.

The parasites do not have it all their own way. The constant war waged against them means they must exist in a certain degree of balance with their hosts, in that if they cause too much irritation their chances of survival are lessened. Simpler parasites such as bacteria and viruses, which we usually term diseases, often fail to maintain this balance and cause death in their hosts, but because of their overwhelming numbers their species survival is little affected.

The worst plague of this kind to affect African wild life was the virus disease cattle plague or rinderpest. From 1889 to 1903 it swept through the length and breadth of Africa, destroying countless numbers of both wild and domestic animals, without a doubt profoundly influencing subsequent survival and distribution patterns of those wild animals that survived. Lord Lugard, travelling through East Africa in 1890, announced that buffalo and eland were almost all gone (the absence of elephant was due to hunting). Subsequent early travellers pessimistically declared the country finished for hunting. Nothing but acre upon acre of bleached skulls bore grim testimony to the ravages of this disease. Fortunately no species seems to have been exterminated, and those badly affected, such as buffalo, made a rapid recovery. The buffalo is said to have regained its former numbers in 30 years, but eland, roan antelope, greater kudu, and lesser kudu have never regained their former densities in East Africa, although the rapid human settlement which followed in the wake of the rinderpest plague may have played a part in this.

Rinderpest then broke out sporadically until it attained a certain degree of equilibrium with its hosts, so the effects were not so disastrous. Although it had been known in Europe and Asia since the Middle Ages, it was suggested that it had never entered Africa before, but this is unlikely in view of its highly contagious nature, so its spread at that time was probably due to the extreme drought conditions that prevailed, causing animals to congregate around dwindling waterholes. Egypt was subject to frequent outbreaks, and the great plague probably had its origin in cattle imported into Egypt, spreading infection to the Sudan where the Mahdi rebellion carried it into Ethiopia. Whatever its origin, it was a horrifying example of how a natural catastrophe could overrun the fauna of an entire continent in the space of a mere 14 years.

Probably every living creature is preyed upon by some parasite or another. I have chosen a mere handful of examples among mammals from a list that would comfortably fill a book of its own. Parasites of fish alone would fill several volumes, and those of birds are legion.

But we cannot leave the subject without mentioning the ostrich, which hosts a tapeworm of which a closely related species parasitizes the South American rhea. Also, and found on no other bird, a feather louse which is very similar; and the West African ostrich shares a species of mite which is the same as that found on the rhea, the only known shared species. The ostrich and its relative the rhea are considered to have originated in Eurasia some 23 million years

Ostriches. They have similar parasites to those of the South American rhea.

ago in the early Miocene, long after the separation of South America from Africa, 100 million years ago. So did the rhea on its migration to South America carry these shared parasites with it? Perhaps, but we cannot rule out the possibility that the Portuguese or the Spanish may have tried to introduce ostriches to South America at some early date in their explorations, which then transferred their parasites to the rhea. Such ostriches would have come from West Africa, and the shared mite suggests this may have been the case. In 1764 several African elephants were shipped from Africa to Villa Rica *de la Vera Cruz (now* Veracruz) in Mexico for use there and in other Spanish American countries, and some zebra were exported to Brazil in the early 19th century, probably from Angola. There is a report of feral ostriches – farmed ostriches that had run wild – existing in New Mexico, but I have not found any confirmation of this.

When this legion of parasites is considered it seems surprising that any animals survive at all in face of such opposition. But as one writer expressed it, 'no organism is an entity unto itself, it lives as a member of a community'. The parasites, as far as they themselves are concerned, are simply taking their rightful place in that community.

11

From swamp to forest: the great diversity of life

The wonderland of African wildlife never ceases to provide surprises. Parasites are bizarre enough for most people, but let us look at some of the less common creatures as well as a few extreme types of adaptation found in Africa's vide variety of habitats.

The aquatic environment is the most prolific of all, and birds are found in profusion on the inland waterways. We see oddities like the saddlebilled stork, with its bill inexplicably painted in the red, black, and yellow of Uganda's national colours. More common is the yellow-billed stork, with a beautiful pink suffusion over its back. It feeds knee-deep in the shallows, performing a ridiculous sort of Charleston; kicking its spindly legs out sideways as it moves along, it holds its beak down between its legs and seizes anything that brushes against them.

Vast numbers of pelicans and cormorants are a sign of a rich supply of fish. Uganda's Lake George, a shallow lake of only 390 square kilometres, was said to be one of the most productive lakes in the world. Formerly this was due in no small measure to fertilization by the large numbers of hippo which deposited countless tonnes of manure into the water after their nightly feeds on land. The result was a rich growth of plankton, as thick as the best green-pea soup, which sparks off a whole chain of life, culminating in fish-eating birds on the one hand and humanity on the other. Humans break the chain by carrying their fish away to eat elsewhere, but the birds add their droppings and their dead bodies back into the cycle.

One of the most extreme habitats from the point of view of animal survival is the swamp, dominated by great masses of papyrus that produce so much carbon dioxide that the water around is acidified and almost devoid of oxygen. But with some 13,000 square kilometres of swamp in Uganda alone, we can expect that some creatures will have developed adaptations to live there. There is a little worm, *Alma*, which sits with its head in the mud and breathes through the tail that it wags above the mud.

[Above] Cormorants indicate a plentiful supply of fish.

[Right] The saddle-billed stork with its bill in Uganda's national colours.

The dweller the swamp usually brings to mind, though, is the sitatunga antelope. Living singly or in pairs, it is more common than generally supposed, but creeps about so furtively in the dense papyrus that it is seldom seen. It is closely related to the bushbuck, and the two are said to have been crossed in captivity. The sitatunga buck has a thick woolly coat, very variable in colour but often very dark. Its horns are attractive, curved like those of the bushbuck, and surmounted with ivory-coloured tips. The hornless doe, rufous with white stripes, is hard to tell apart at first glance from the bushbuck. The interest of the sitatunga is in its feet, with its 15 cm splayed hooves that enable it to walk over floating vegetation. Even so, it cannot move fast but leaps clumsily from clump to clump, pausing to select its next landing place at each leap, but as it is an adept swimmer it doesn't matter much if it does fall into the water. Sitatunga used to be very numerous on islands in Lake Victoria, but most were eliminated in the anti-sleeping sickness measures. On one island they had reverted to life on dry land and lost their overgrown hooves, on another they were so plentiful and tame the missionary had to drive them out of his mission hall before he could start his services. The natives say the antelope can imitate the noise of a hippo. This was confirmed by a game warden who told me he once heard what he took to be a hippo grunting, but stalking to the edge of a pool found only a sitatunga there.

Another antelope of the swamps is the lechwe, also with splayed hooves to help it walk over the reeds, but not as splayed out as those of the sitatunga. A handsome dark-coloured species occurs in the dense swamps, the Sudd, of the Nile, and then they are not found again until we reach the backbone of central Africa, missing out eastern and western Africa completely, but occurring from Zambia into Botswana. Of a golden colour it looks much like a kob, the does hornless but the bucks with large, lyrate horns; it can occur in immense herds numbering many thousands. Strangely enough, from the Nile to southern Africa it hosts a warble fly which

[Above] The red lechwe, a swamp-dwelling antelope.

[Left] Red lechwe.

125

A puku buck in Botswana. Puku were once numerous.

must have adapted its lifecycle to pupate when the lechwe is on dry land, for it would not do its chances of survival much good if it emerged from under the skin to pupate only to fall into the water.

Restricted to the edges of swamps in a few localities in southern Africa is the puku, also rufous with moderate horns in the buck, looking much like a kob. The great hunter Selous encountered them in large numbers in Botswana in the 19th century, but today their numbers are low.

Another oddity of the swamps is the great, bizarre-looking shoebill, or whale-headed stork. It occasionally visits the fringes of swamps, where one may be lucky enough to see it. A strictly African bird, it is about the size of a marabou stork, but smoky grey. It has a large, curiously-shaped bill, reminiscent of a Dutch clog. The bill seems to be adapted for catching lungfish, which it achieves by making a sort of belly-flop onto the water from a standing position, seizing the fish as they surface to breathe. As it breeds far out in the swamps, its nest is rarely seen. Ornithologists are undecided whether to call it a stork, a heron, or a pelican. While it is normally a silent, mournful bird, captive specimens greet their keepers by chattering their beak like a stork. But experiments have shown that when suffering heat stress they pant, fluttering their throat like a heron or a pelican, whereas storks squirt urine over their legs, the evaporation being said to cool them. This is why the legs of the marabou stork are often so white, looking as if they are wearing an American Marine's gaiters.

The air-breathing lungfish, which can grow bigger than a human and must come to the surface to breathe, rapidly gulping a mouthful of air as it flips over, diving back down again almost instantaneously, has no difficulty in the swamps. If the water dries up it buries itself in the mud. Making a hard cocoon around itself it, waits for the next rains to release it again. These aestivating burrows, as they are termed, are rare in Uganda, but I was lucky enough to find some near Lake Edward. When I returned later I found that some animal, probably a hyaena, had also found them and dug out all of the fish. A lungfish is no mean adversary, for it has a vicious rat-trap jaw arrayed with teeth like a leopard's. If captured it opens its mouth in readiness to bite and actually grunts a warning at you.

The catfish, whose migratory habits I have already described, is also an air-breather, and if it cannot reach the surface to breathe it drowns. But instead of a lung like the lungfish, it has a delicate pink, sponge-like outgrowth of the gills, adapted for breathing air. It is a voracious feeder and when watching some of them feeding in the shallows I saw one throw itself onto land, wrestling with some overhanging roots. Seemingly the most normal thing in the world for a fish to do, it simply wriggled back to the edge and plopped back into the water. I once watched several of these fish converge upon one point in a little backwater, and the next moment a 20 cm tilapia leapt out of the water over their backs, escaping to safety. Had I witnessed a conscious method of co-operative fishing akin to that of the orca? Or was it simply incidental, the catfish being attracted to any disturbance?

Like the catfish, many aquatic inhabitants use temporary bodies of water for egg-laying, as the number of aquatic predators is then reduced. This is fine if the eggs can develop before the pool dries out. Frogs and toads are well-known examples of creatures that use this method. The first rains herald a deafening cacophony of boisterous croaking in the African night. If

Lungfish in threatening pose.

you should happen upon a pool just at the right time you will find congregating toads in their thousands, all drawn together by the nuptial song. How a toad knows which way to go when calls are coming from all directions at once is a mystery to me, but somehow every pool and puddle gets occupied. The period of pairing and egg-laying is brief, lasting not more than a day or two, for already the storm-troopers are massing; storks, herons, birds of prey, monitor lizards, and snakes, all move in to gorge themselves. The toads only escape much of this onslaught by being nocturnal. Within hours they have dispersed, leaving their eggs behind them.

Most creatures that I have discussed are equally at home in more friendly aquatic habitats than papyrus swamps and temporary pools, but there is one watery medium that requires extreme specialization indeed. This is the soda lake.

The flamingo's association with this habitat has already been mentioned, but more remarkable is the adaptation shown by two little tilapia fishes, each less than 8 cm long. One, *Tilapia grahami*, lives in Lake Magadi, and the other, *Tilapia alcalia*, in Lake Natron, both in Kenya. These lakes are very alkaline with hot springs, and not only can these fish withstand the high soda content but they can withstand the hot water as well. Feeding on algae, as do the flamingos, they swim right into the hot springs, where the temperature, at 43°C, is several degrees above lethal; the limit most fish can withstand is 30°C. But in the hot water the algae grow in profusion, and the tilapia survive by swimming through these lethal temperatures to reach the cold shallows for breeding.

A large part of East Africa is arid. Rainfall is scarce, and desert or near-desert conditions exist. Here the adaptations of animals are mostly to conserve water, a physiological problem not often betrayed by their outward appearance. Animals like the gerenuk, with its long neck enabling it to reach a wide range of browse, and the oryx are able to exist without water for long periods. Water is lost from the body by sweating, in urine, in faeces, and via respiration, and the gerenuk and the oryx reduce those forms of water loss. The waterbuck, however, is unable to control these losses, so it needs to drink almost three times as much water as the oryx.

The easiest way to avoid heat in an arid environment is to live underground. Perhaps the most specialized mammal of Africa's dry regions is the naked mole rat, an odd, embryonic-looking creature, naked but for a few scattered light hairs. Almost blind, it has minute eyes – but this is no disadvantage in its wholly subterranean existence. An industrious burrower, it lives in colonies of up to 100 animals. Other than its lack of hair it is not unlike the common mole rat, which is so numerous in parts of Kenya that its molehills make the ground look as if it had been ploughed. The common mole rat lives in the open savannah grassland with its scattered trees and bush, a somewhat friendlier environment than its naked cousin.

The largest type of habitat in East Africa – the open grassland plains with their scattered trees and bush – undergo marked seasonal changes: dry as a desert at the end of the dry season, and wet as a sponge, with sodden, waterlogged plains, at the end of the wet. This is the home of almost all the larger game animals. When seasons are good they can increase apace in number, but if the dry season is long they pay a heavy toll. Hippos can travel long distances overland and inhabit pools far from permanent water. That's all right in the wet season, but I came across such an isolated pool in Tanzania's Rukwa Valley at the height of a prolonged drought. Hundreds of hippo were crammed into the remains of a pool in a dry streambed, now nothing

[Left] Mole rat. A rodent of the savannah.

[Below] Hippos in mud in a drying wallow.

more than mud. There was no food for them in the surrounding dried-up plain, and although they got some solace from the mud in which they lay packed like sardines, they were completely exposed to the relentless sun without shade of any description.

Did they try to find water? Or did they all die there of heat exhaustion, starvation, and thirst?

Only in more recent years have we begun to appreciate how, and why, this great variety of animals that we find is able to exist together. If there is enough food we meet two broad divisions: numbers of few large species, or numbers of many smaller species.

In western Uganda and the eastern Congo we find the first category. Some 50 years ago there were great herds of buffalo 500 strong, incredible populations of hippo, numbering up to 27 per square kilometre along rivers and lake fringes, and huge armies of elephants. All this added up in kilograms per square kilometre to a tremendous weight of meat, all tied up in relatively few species. Some animals, like the reedbuck, are now few in number; others, such as impala, zebra, and eland, absent altogether. In most of Kenya and Tanzania we find a much greater variety of species that use the habitat more effectively. Their weight, distributed between zebra, wildebeest, and other antelopes, probably adds up to just as much given equal conditions. These families of species can exist together because on the whole they do not compete with one another.

The bull giraffe builds up his 1.5 tonnes by cropping foliage that no other animal except the elephant can reach. Where giraffes are numerous their industrious topiary makes the thorn trees look as if they have been trimmed with shears. Widemouthed grazers like buffalo can pull in mouthfuls of tussocky grass, but slender-muzzled antelopes like the Tommy must pick their food more delicately. Hippos are almost entirely grazers, using their broad horny lips to crop grass as efficiently as a lawnmower, but, strangely enough, have also been known to feed upon rotting carcasses of their own kind. Some herbivores feed on different stages of plant growth, whilst others mix grazing with browsing. Much overlap in food preferences occurs, more so than we used to like to think, but overall a balance is struck. This enables many different animals to mingle in harmony, conscious of the fact that they are not outright competitors.

This harmony extends to the relation with carnivores, except for the elephant, which works itself up into a fury when it scents a lion – and it is not very tolerant towards other animals, either. Contrary to the belief of the ancients expressed by Pliny that 'towards weaker animals they show compassion', the elephant does not tolerate any animal remaining in its path. An angry swishing of its trunk is more likely to wallop any sheep out of its path than to gently lift it aside, as Pliny supposed.

But the real battles of nature are fought down at the feet of the larger animals. The grassland jungle where insect eats insect is even more intricate and throbbing with life than the world a few feet above. During the dry season, when the earth is almost bare, things quieten down, but with the first rains it bursts into life. One of the first insects to visit the puddles is the warningly-coloured black and yellow female mud wasp, *Scoliphron spirifex*. Walking onto the mud, and somehow never dirtying herself, she rolls a little mud into a perfect ball. This done, she flies away with it to build a sausage-shaped cocoon in which she lays an egg, and then proceeds to stuff the cocoon with paralysed spiders and other insects. Each time the mud wasp flies back with more food she breaks open the entrance, continually emitting a high-pitched whine, perhaps to indicate that she is not a predator. After each visit she neatly plasters the entrance up again. The amount of food she leaves determines the size of her offspring; if you remove most of it, what will emerge is a miniature of the parent!

Should you be walking through the grassland when the ground is damp from the first rains, you may hear a squeaking noise coming from the ground at your feet. Don't be alarmed;

[Right] A mud wasp bringing food to its cocoon.

[Lower right] Dung beetle with grub and dung balls. The balls are larger than a tennis ball.

it's only the dung beetle, *Heliocopris dilloni*, emerging from its underground prison, squeaking joyfully at its liberation. These large, 5-cm-long beetles, do not roll their ball of dung away searching for a soft burying place; they burrow immediately beneath the dung pile, heaping the excavated earth up over it like a molehill. The dung can be taken down nearly a metre, where this extraordinarily industrious beetle proceeds to fashion it into half a dozen or more balls the size of a fist. These it coats with a smooth, half-inch-thick, perfectly spherical layer of hardened earth to stop the contents drying out, leaving a neat little fibrous breathing plug at one point. It achieves all of this underground. The egg that has been ensconced in each ball hatches into an ugly-looking white grub. This proceeds to eat its way through the meal of dung. Whether it finishes just in time for the rains, or whether it knows the rains have begun, is another mystery to me. The adult is a noisy creature at the best of times. If you pick one up it protests with a noise just like a clockwork toy. The undersides usually carry a few mites that hitch a lift to dung piles.

Dung beetles, or scarab beetles, were worshipped by the Ancient Egyptians, believing that a giant one rolled the sun across the sky. The dung, which the scarabs find by scent, is patted into a ball with specially modified front legs. It is noted for making a dung ball of up to 40 times its own weight and then rolling it away to find a burial place of its choice. It does not push the ball with its front legs but always with its back legs, rolling it up Lilliputian hill and down Lilliputian dale, stumbling and recovering itself with a mad intensity of purpose, like Sisyphus. the ancient Greek condemned to forever rolling a huge round stone up a mountain, which, whenever he got it to the top, rolled back down again. The animal artist Edmund Caldwell made a famous error when he illustrated Sir Percy Fitzpatrick's *Jock of the Bushveld* 1907 with a sketch of a dung beetle pushing its ball with its front feet; this was hastily corrected in the next printing. Speed in hiding the ball seems to be the beetle's aim. These surface-rolling beetles bury the ball only a few centimetres underground. Little wonder. They are probably too exhausted to do more. Sometimes a second beetle will join in, appearing to co-operate in the task – but in fact it is trying to steal the other's ball. These balls, having been buried, may then be eaten at leisure. When the female is going to use one to feed her young she makes a much bigger underground chamber and, having produced a rounded ball to her satisfaction, makes a hollow on one side and deposits an egg in it, then builds the dung up around it so that the egg is in a hollow, pear-shaped projection, where it eventually hatches. The fat white grub then eats its way through the inside of the dung ball until it is ensconced in a hollow shell. It then pupates, emerging as an adult about a month later.

By burying the dung before it has time to dry out, dung beetles play an important part in an environment where worms are few. Just how important has been realised in Australia where there were no such beetles and the outback was gradually becoming buried under dung, which in that environment dries out so rapidly that little decomposition can take place. African dung beetles have been introduced to deal with this.

The striking rhinoceros beetles with their enormous horns are less often seen, and less welcome. The adult is a pest of palm trees, feeding on the young unopened shoots. When the frond uncurls it looks as if someone has been playing scissor games with it. The larvae live in decaying vegetation, rotting trees, and compost heaps.

Many grassland insects prey upon one another as well as being preyed upon themselves by birds and reptiles, and extraordinary adaptations have been evolved to eat, or to avoid being eaten. A little thornbug, for example, looks exactly like the triple thorns of the *Acacia senegal* tree. When I found one I would not have known the difference had not the thorns moved. These bugs are attended by ants that stroke them with their antennae to obtain liquid that they produce from their hind ends, rather like ants and aphids in temperate zones.

Best-known of the predatory insects is the praying mantis, which to deceive its prey adopts many disguises, looking like anything from a blade of grass to a piece of grey lichen. They are widespread around the world, with several thousand species. The one that looks like a piece of lichen has a counterpart in Florida, USA, living more or less the same lifestyle. Voracious carnivores, in Africa feeding on other insects, the mantis has distinctive large front legs specially adapted for seizing prey, holding them together (hence the moniker 'praying') before it is ready to pounce, and a triangular head with large eyes. In South America the larger species attack small birds, lizards, and frogs.

Most insects cannot turn their heads, but the mantis can swivel its head around, waving like a leaf, to look behind it as it stalks slowly through the grass. Because she can swivel her head

[Left] Rhinoceros beetle.

[Right] A thorn bug.

around, the larger female will eat the male during pairing if she can seize it – but even if his head is eaten off the mating continues as it is controlled by the male's hinder end, and in fact is stimulated by the loss of his head. The female only does this, however, if the male does not seize her properly, otherwise mating takes place without hindrance. The paper-like egg cases of the mantis, some of which look like little Chinese lanterns, may often be found gummed to grass stalks in the savannah. The number of stages the emergent mantis must pass through to attain adulthood varies from three to as many as twelve, taking about a year to complete.

There are three groups of the extraordinary stick insects: the giant, the grass, and the leaf, known as *Phasmida*, from the Latin for 'apparition'. The crafty stick insect is solely a plant eater, adopting its camouflage because it is so helpless, slow-moving as it is; most cannot fly, and none can jump. If touched it freezes to escape detection, with its long front legs held out stiffly before it, an instinctive reaction. I once found grass stick insects all climbing trees after dark; dozens were climbing the trunks to roost above the ground. Apparently they feed after dark; after all, it's not much advantage being disguised as something to escape predators if its disguise cannot be seen in the dark. The largest, the female giant *Palophus* (*Bactrododema*) *reyi*, reaches a length of over 40 cm with her legs stretched out in front and behind, making her among the longest of all insects, pride of place going to a specimen from Borneo. The much smaller male has hind wings which enable slow flight, but in the female they are too small, so when alarmed

 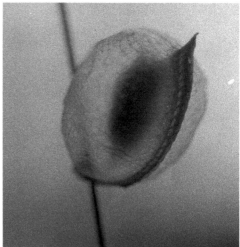

[Left] A praying mantis disguised as lichen.

[Right] Praying mantis egg case.

she raises them and flaps them, making a rustling sound to try and scare off predators. The male is often found clinging to the female.

A peculiarity is that in some species – one such occurs in south-west Africa – the female does not require a mate but lays exclusively female eggs without mating; parthenogenesis. In others males occur but are uncommon, the female producing eggs without a male for generation after generation until, in adverse conditions such as lack of food, males are produced and pairing then takes place. When it does, it lasts for several hours. In the giant and in the leaf the female is twice the size of the male. The eggs, which look like bird droppings, hatch into tiny replicas of the parent female which have to change their skin five or six times before becoming fully adult. Once the skin has been shed, the owner, after resting, eats it. Before it is adult, if it loses a limb it produces a new stump at the next moult, which increases in size with each successive moult.

The mantis and the stick insect are allied to the locusts and grasshoppers, the latter of interest in that they match their colour to the background. Thus they are green when the vegetation is green in the wet season, straw-coloured when the vegetation is brown in the dry season, and black after the seasonal grass fires. Some can effect a colour change in two days. Not all species can do this, however, and some adopt a compromise colour. William Burchell, an explorer in South Africa, was apparently the first to notice this colour change in 1814, giving the specimens he collected the name of *Gryllus chameleon*, but noting that they could not change colour rapidly like a chameleon. In Britain we have a straw-coloured and a green phase, but not the fire phase. Many other insects also adopt a black phase to match burnt surroundings.

This camouflage is necessary because hunting the insects are many birds that live in the open grasslands. A common species is the little zitting cisticola, named from the peculiar

[Clockwise from above]

A stick insect mimics a blade of grass.

Zitting cisticola, a bird of the grassland.

Section of a zitting cisticola's nest.

rattling sound it makes with its wings when in flight. A small bird, it builds a beautiful flask-shaped nest lined with spiders' webs and cleverly concealed in the grass. Another bird nesting in the grass, making a round ball of a nest, is the little plum-coloured fire finch, described as looking like an animated plum; unfortunately for it, it is a great favourite with cage bird enthusiasts. Common in the grass in parts of Uganda is the tiny button quail. The chicks are incredibly minute balls of fluff that scamper cheeping after their parents, looking like furry marbles on legs. So small are they that you could comfortably house two in a small matchbox.

Some birds that are not themselves protectively coloured choose quite open ground for nesting. This way they can spot any predators creeping up on them. A good example is the wattled plover; I once found its nest made out of the middle of a dried buffalo pat. This bird sits very tight when nesting, and will even make a threat display at a Land rover! I watched one threaten an inquisitive baby topi, spreading its wings in defiance, but this only made the baby topi more curious, until it suddenly scampered off, perhaps from a peck on the nose.

[Left] Wattled plover with its nest in a dried buffalo pat.

[Below] Wattled plover nesting in the open on the dried buffalo pat nest.

A remarkable association exists between a nondescript brown bird called the honeyguide, *Indicator indicator*, and its craving for honey and bee grubs. The bird finds the bees' nests and then guides another honey-lover – the ratel, or honey badger – to them, and shares the spoils that the ratel digs out – with its thick skin, it is impervious to the attacks of the bees. If the honeyguide cannot find a ratel to take with it, then it looks for a human. Although I was once rather sceptical of the truth of this I had to alter my opinion when I lived in the Akagera National Park; during the flowering season of the acacia trees when the bees were nesting I could hardly travel anywhere, whether on foot or in a Land rover, without being accosted by one of these birds. Soon I would hear the bird's insistent chitter and see it flitting from bush to bush. I tried following one once, and it merely led me around aimlessly – but the African guides often came back laden with honey thanks to the honeyguide's generosity. One of the birds even came to my house and set up a persistent nagging, perched in the garden hedge for two days, but no one would answer its call because it was too late in the season and there would be only grubs in the nest. Tradition has it that you must always leave the honeyguide some of the spoils, otherwise next time it will lead you to something nasty, like a snake or a rhino.

Insects eating insects, birds eating insects, and of course birds eating birds ... the African savannah accommodates the greatest variety of birds of prey in the world, from the insectivorous pygmy falcon to the great martial eagle, most powerful of them all. Perched

Martial eagle.

[Above] Vultures.

[Right] Kori bustard.

disdainfully in a favourite thorn tree it allows a close approach, deigning to stay unmoved. The martial eagle, like that other beauty of the skies, the bateleur eagle, will take young antelopes, but most birds of prey feed on lizards, snakes, rodents, and other small birds. But the most common large birds are the scavengers, the vultures, which feed upon the remains of the predator's prey or upon animals that have died from some other cause. They find them by their remarkable eyesight, trawling the skies so high up that to the onlooker they are mere specks. But a patch of flattened vegetation or a body will attract them, sometimes within minutes.

You may encounter the kori bustard, the largest flying bird in Africa, stalking imperiously across the plain. Not a bird of prey, but nevertheless a scourge of snakes and rodents.

The forest regions of East Africa are not extensive, and what there was has been sadly reduced in the last 100 years by clearing and fire. Most of the energy of the forest environment is tied up in tall trees, and there is little weight of animals, or biomass as the scientist calls it. The birds and mammals are shy and secretive. Unless you sit quietly and patiently you do not see them but you hear them, for the forest is a tremendously noisy place. A continuous hum of bird song and insects, dominated above all by the unending penetrating shrill of the male cicada.

Nothing more than a giant plant bug, the 5 cm cicada, reveals itself only at the beginning of the rains, when it may be seen whirring clumsily from tree to tree. Over 1,500 species of cicada exist, extending as far north as England's New Forest. But the English ones are not half as big and noisy as their African cousins. They are the noisiest of all the insects, and their shrill, deafening sound, its purpose to attract the mute female, is made by a muscular vibration of two shell-like drums. Henri Fabre, the famous French entomologist, concluded that cicadas were deaf, as when he fired a cannon under a tree in which some were singing they continued without pause. We now know that they can hear, but probably switch off when singing. Nevertheless they are very hard to find when not swarming, as if you walk near to them they stop singing.

The best way to see a forest mammal is to wait by a salt-lick or a watering spot. Always on the alert, these mammals are seldom seen by anyone moving. The elusive bongo, the most rarely seen of any African antelope except at favoured salt-licks, gave me a good demonstration of this. I had already made several unsuccessful trips to such a salt-lick in Kenya's Cherangani hills. Early one morning I sat cramped and cold in a hide, staring into the misty tangle of lichen-draped boughs when one suddenly appeared. I turned my head and there he was, standing suspiciously, a large, handsome, rufous and white-striped animal, with white-tipped, bushbuck-like horns. Alert for the slightest hint of danger, he stood motionless a full 15 minutes, with only slight movements of the head. A rustle here, a tiny noise there, and he turned eyes and ears this way and that, searching the forest gloom for danger. He moved forward slightly, now in full view as I crouched uncomfortably in the hide. He stood yet another 15 minutes, silent, suspicious, trumpet-like ears twitching, his nose questing the air currents. And then abruptly he turned and melted away without a sound. Little wonder the bongo is so seldom seen!

The last large mammal in Africa to be made known to science, the giant forest hog, was not discovered until 1904. (The bonobo was known before that, but not distinguished from other chimpanzees until the 1920s.) The hog is now known to be common in many forests, though seldom seen. Fat as a barrel, a fully-grown boar weighs up to 270 kilos. It is jet black, with two great 'warts' in front of the eyes but small tushes. Usually preferring forest, in western Uganda it extends its range into scrub and may sometimes be met with first thing in the morning out in the open. Sometimes it even allows you to get quite close, staring in surprise at you before turning tail and diving headlong into the bush.

Giant forest hog.

Bushpig.

The red river hog or bushpig is another forest pig. Unlike the others it is handsome to look at, the sow bright red with white side-whiskers. The boar is darker and can weigh about 90 kilos. In some areas it is so common as to be a serious pest but rarely seen. My closest encounter was when one ran into the side of my Land rover. It was a solitary specimen that had somehow got mixed up with some warthog running about in the open. I had tried to cut it off to take a photograph, but instead of turning aside it kept straight on, skidding into the side of the vehicle. I was too surprised to take a picture.

In contrast to the stealth of many forest animals, monkeys and chimpanzees are amongst the noisiest of creatures. Monkeys use their arms as legs, or brachiate, as the scientist terms it, swinging through the branches of the tall trees where scent is of little use but acute eyesight is. But vision, too, is limited in the leafy canopy, so calling becomes important in keeping the animals together – or apart, as the case may be. Most of these primates rarely come to the ground, except for the chimpanzee; on the forest floor it moves faster and feels safer than in the trees. Whenever you stalk chimpanzees they do not disappear by leaping through the branches; they climb to the ground and run away on all fours. Anyone who has visited a zoo knows that chimpanzees are capable of the most blood-curdling screams and 'hoo-hooing' calls, and when you are in the forest alone with them this can be quite intimidating. Once, when I was stalking chimpanzees in Uganda's Maramagambo Forest with a companion, and we halted, uncertain which way to continue, suddenly a terrifying clamour of screaming and tree-drumming, the latter made by the chimpanzee beating the bole of a tree with its palms, burst out a few yards away in the undergrowth. We stood, half-expecting to be attacked, when an answering clamour erupted immediately behind us. We were obviously well and truly surrounded, but could see nothing. Its suddenness and volume certainly served the purpose of causing some momentary alarm, but on our pressing forward in the direction of the last sound this put them to flight without giving us even a glimpse.

Several instances of chimpanzees attacking people have, however, been reported from the area. Women drawing water have been assaulted by old males (it seems because the women were blocking the chimpanzees' route, not for any other reason), and road workers have even threatened strike action because chimpanzees kept menacing them. A scientist friend once had to retreat before an advance of chimpanzees when he was trapping rodents in the forest. But if

The chimpanzee is at home in the treetops.

you stalk them the tables are turned; they become extremely shy and you are lucky to even see them.

So much now is known about the gorilla, particularly the mountain gorilla, that it is familiar to all who watch television; but they were once not so readily seen and in areas where they have not become accustomed to tourists they are still elusive. There, all you are likely to hear is the bark of the male as he makes his departure, or perhaps you can glimpse a patch of black hair vanishing into the forest. Due to their weight they are more ground-dwelling than tree-dwelling, but the youngsters enjoy climbing about in the trees. Gorillas build nests in low shrubs to sleep at night, a few branches being bent and beaten together into a low depression, and during the day they wander leisurely through the forest undergrowth, feeding on the vegetation.

Rarely seen because of its nocturnal habits is a cuddly little creature called the potto, although it is not as gentle as it looks. The potto feeds on birds and fruit, seizing the former with its sharp canine teeth that can bite through a fingernail, as a friend of mine discovered. It

A nocturnal animal, the potto.

can move much more quickly than is generally believed, but normally moves along a branch rather like a chameleon, one foot in the air at a time. This prevents the branch shaking and may be associated with the potto's habit of catching roosting birds. A peculiarity of the potto is its neck vertebrae, which have prominent spines projecting up under the skin. It has always been supposed that these were for protection but their purpose seems to be exactly the opposite. The spines are very sensitive and when two friendly pottos meet they bow towards one another like Manchurian noblemen, and rub the backs of their necks together.

So the way to befriend a potto is to rub the spines gently with your finger. But charming as pottos are to look at, it is said that you can never tame them. When they grow up their vulnerability seems to make them very irritable and if handled they start biting, nipping gently at first, but becoming more and more aggressive until released. They also have the habit of marking everything with urine – even you, if they like you – just like bushbabies, which are also rarely seen.

Many other small creatures inhabit the forest. Squirrels are plentiful, from the ground to the bushes to the trees, so are one of the most likely mammals to be seen. But despite their charming appearance many carry a virus fatal to humans. There is a cuddly grey dormouse with a bushy tail that makes it look like a miniature squirrel. Less common is the palm civet, a catlike creature much like a genet but with skid pads on its paws. This must mean it is a good climber.

It is somewhat similar in appearance to the much more common genet cat, a delightful tabby-coloured creature with a long tail. Although they are creatures of the bush, they can make delightful pets and can even be housetrained to use a toilet for their droppings. I once tried taking the photograph of a young tame one by placing it on top of an anthill and then running back to the camera that I had set up on a tripod. But the genet thought this was a great game and every time I turned and ran for the camera it bounded after me, thinking it was some sort of race, going into paroxysms of excitement as I tried to run faster and faster. In the end it did stop long enough for me to get a picture. Charming as they are, they are hated by people who keep chickens, and get short shrift from the Africans.

If you are lucky you may see a serval, most dainty of all the cats. Usually nocturnal, it sometimes lingers long enough to be seen in the early morning. It is also just as much at home on the savannah.

The African forest holds many secrets, and there are still new discoveries to be made. Is the winged pterodactyl-like reptile, 'as big as a ram', as described in Angola in the 16th century,

Ground squirrel.

[From top]

African dormouse.

Bush squirrel. It lacks the characteristic side stripe of the ground squirrel.

[Clockwise from top left]

Genet cat.

The palm civet.

Serval cat. It hunts during
the day as well as at night.

Sunset in Uganda.

extinct? The same writer described a peacock there, the Congo peacock, which was not rediscovered until 1936.

When the farmer envies the sleek and immaculate appearance of the zebra roaming the plains, he should reflect that this appearance is not akin to that of a pampered prize bull or stallion. It is instead the culmination of a thousand and one interacting causes. Predators have removed the weak and the not-so-sleek, and the zebra is assured a supply of food because what it eats has been dictated by the co-ordinated evolution of the whole community, a tangled web of life that found its origin over 300 million years ago. I hope in these pages I have conveyed some idea of just how wonderful, intricate, and diverse that community is, enriching the world that we live in today.

An African time chart

Period	Millions of years ago	Remarks
Quaternary Pleistocene	2.6	Age of mammals, wet and dry fluctuations
Tertiary Pliocene	5	Obscure in East Africa
Miocene.	23	First East African Tertiary deposits
Oligocene	34	Many mammals in Egyptian deposits
Eocene	56	Elephants, sirenia, and hyraces in Egypt
Palaeocene	66	No African fossil record
Secondary Cretaceous	145	
Jurassic	200	Movement of continents begins
.	201	Dinosaurs at Tendaguru
Triassic	252	First true mammals appear
Primary Permian	299	Pareiasaurs appear, first African fossils
Carboniferous	359	Glaciation in Africa
Devonian	419	Age of fishes
Silurian	444	
Ordovician	485	
Cambrian	541	
Precambrian	4567